FTCE Physics 6-12
Teacher Certification Exam

By: Sharon A. Wynne, M.S.

XAMonline, Inc.
Boston

To obtain permission(s) to use the material from this work for any purpose including workshops or seminars, please submit a written request to:

XAMonline, Inc.
21 Orient Avenue
Melrose, MA 02176
Toll Free 1-800-301-4647
Email: info@xamonline.com
Web www.xamonline.com

Library of Congress Cataloging-in-Publication Data
Wynne, Sharon A.

    FTCE Physics 6-12: Teacher Certification / Sharon A. Wynne.
    ISBN 978-1-64239-014-8

1. Physics 6-12   2. Study Guides.   3. FTCE
4. Teachers' Certification & Licensure.   5. Careers

Disclaimer:

The opinions expressed in this publication are the sole works of XAMonline and were created independently from the National Education Association, Educational Testing Service, or any State Department of Education, National Evaluation Systems or other testing affiliates.

Between the time of publication and printing, state specific standards as well as testing formats and website information may change that is not included in part or in whole within this product. XAMonline developed the sample test questions and the questions reflect similar content as on real tests; however, they are not former tests. XAMonline assembles content that aligns with state standards but makes no claims nor guarantees teacher candidates a passing score. Numerical scores are determined by testing companies such as NES or ETS and then are compared with individual state standards. A passing score varies from state to state.

Printed in the United States of America

FTCE: Physics 6-12
ISBN: 978-1-64239-014-8

Table of Contents

COMPETENCY V.   KNOWLEDGE OF VIBRATIONS, WAVES, AND SOUND

COMPETENCY VIII.   KNOWLEDGE OF MODERN PHYSICS

Great Study and Testing Tips!

What to study in order to prepare for the subject assessments is the focus of this study guide but equally important is *how* you study.

You can increase your chances of truly mastering the information by taking some simple, but effective steps.

Study Tips:

1. **Some foods aid the learning process**. Foods such as milk, nuts, seeds, rice, and oats help your study efforts by releasing natural memory enhancers called CCKs (*cholecystokinin*) composed of *tryptopha*n, *choline*, and *phenylalanine*. All of these chemicals enhance the neurotransmitters associated with memory. Before studying, try a light, protein-rich meal of eggs, turkey, and fish. All of these foods release the memory enhancing chemicals. The better the connections, the more you comprehend.

Likewise, before you take a test, stick to a light snack of energy boosting and relaxing foods. A glass of milk, a piece of fruit, or some peanuts all release various memory-boosting chemicals and help you to relax and focus on the subject at hand.

2. **Learn to take great notes.** A by-product of our modern culture is that we have grown accustomed to getting our information in short doses (i.e. TV news sound bites or USA Today style newspaper articles.)

Consequently, we've subconsciously trained ourselves to assimilate information better in neat little packages. If your notes are scrawled all over the paper, it fragments the flow of the information. Strive for clarity. Newspapers use a standard format to achieve clarity. Your notes can be much clearer through use of proper formatting. A very effective format is called the *"Cornell Method."*

> Take a sheet of loose-leaf lined notebook paper and draw a line all the way down the paper about 1-2" from the left-hand edge.

> Draw another line across the width of the paper about 1-2" up from the bottom. Repeat this process on the reverse side of the page.

Look at the highly effective result. You have ample room for notes, a left hand margin for special emphasis items or inserting supplementary data from the textbook, a large area at the bottom for a brief summary, and a little rectangular space for just about anything you want.

3. Get the concept then the details. Too often we focus on the details and don't gather an understanding of the concept. However, if you simply memorize only dates, places, or names, you may well miss the whole point of the subject.

A key way to understand things is to put them in your own words. If you are working from a textbook, automatically summarize each paragraph in your mind. If you are outlining text, don't simply copy the author's words.

Rephrase them in your own words. You remember your own thoughts and words much better than someone else's, and subconsciously tend to associate the important details to the core concepts.

4. Ask Why? Pull apart written material paragraph by paragraph and don't forget the captions under the illustrations.

Example: If the heading is "Stream Erosion", flip it around to read "Why do streams erode?" Then answer the questions.

If you train your mind to think in a series of questions and answers, not only will you learn more, but it also helps to lessen the test anxiety because you are used to answering questions.

5. Read for reinforcement and future needs. Even if you only have 10 minutes, put your notes or a book in your hand. Your mind is similar to a computer; you have to input data in order to have it processed. *By reading, you are creating the neural connections for future retrieval.* The more times you read something, the more you reinforce the learning of ideas.

Even if you don't fully understand something on the first pass, *your mind stores much of the material for later recall.*

6. Relax to learn so go into exile. Our bodies respond to an inner clock called biorhythms. Burning the midnight oil works well for some people, but not everyone.

If possible, set aside a particular place to study that is free of distractions. Shut off the television, cell phone, and pager and exile your friends and family during your study period.

If you really are bothered by silence, try background music. Light classical music at a low volume has been shown to aid in concentration over other types. Music that evokes pleasant emotions without lyrics is highly suggested. Try just about anything by Mozart. It relaxes you.

7. <u>**Use arrows not highlighters.**</u> At best, it's difficult to read a page full of yellow, pink, blue, and green streaks. Try staring at a neon sign for a while and you'll soon see that the horde of colors obscure the message.

A quick note, a brief dash of color, an underline, and an arrow pointing to a particular passage is much clearer than a horde of highlighted words.

8. <u>**Budget your study time.**</u> Although you shouldn't ignore any of the material, *allocate your available study time in the same ratio that topics may appear on the test.*

Testing Tips:

1. Get smart, play dumb. Don't read anything into the question. Don't make an assumption that the test writer is looking for something else than what is asked. Stick to the question as written and don't read extra things into it.

2. Read the question and all the choices *twice* before answering the question. You may miss something by not carefully reading, and then re-reading both the question and the answers.

If you really don't have a clue as to the right answer, leave it blank on the first time through. Go on to the other questions, as they may provide a clue as to how to answer the skipped questions.

If later on, you still can't answer the skipped ones . . . *Guess.* The only penalty for guessing is that you *might* get it wrong. Only one thing is certain; if you don't put anything down, you will get it wrong!

3. Turn the question into a statement. Look at the way the questions are worded. The syntax of the question usually provides a clue. Does it seem more familiar as a statement rather than as a question? Does it sound strange?

By turning a question into a statement, you may be able to spot if an answer sounds right, and it may also trigger memories of material you have read.

4. Look for hidden clues. It's actually very difficult to compose multiple-foil (choice) questions without giving away part of the answer in the options presented.

In most multiple-choice questions you can often readily eliminate one or two of the potential answers. This leaves you with only two real possibilities and automatically your odds go to Fifty-Fifty for very little work.

5. Trust your instincts. For every fact that you have read, you subconsciously retain something of that knowledge. On questions that you aren't really certain about, go with your basic instincts. **Your first impression on how to answer a question is usually correct.**

6. Mark your answers directly on the test booklet. Don't bother trying to fill in the optical scan sheet on the first pass through the test.
Just be very careful not to miss-mark your answers when you eventually transcribe them to the scan sheet.

7. Watch the clock! You have a set amount of time to answer the questions. Don't get bogged down trying to answer a single question at the expense of 10 questions you can more readily answer.

COMPETENCY I. KNOWLEDGE OF THE BASIC NATURE OF PHYSICS

Skill 1.1 Identify the components of the scientific method (e.g., assumptions, observations, hypotheses, conclusions, laws, theories).

The scientific method is just a logical set of steps that a scientist goes through to solve a problem. There are as many different scientific methods as there are scientists experimenting. However, there seems to be some pattern to their work.

A law is the highest-level of certainty science can achieve followed by theories and hypothesis. The scientific method is the process by which data is collected, interpreted and validated.

Law: A law is a statement of an order or relation of phenomena that, as far as is known, is invariable under the given conditions. Everything we observe in the universe operates according to known natural laws.

- If the truth of a statement is verified repeatedly in a reproducible way then it can reach the level of a natural law.
- Some well known and accepted natural laws of science are:

1.   The First Law of Thermodynamics

2.   The Second Law of Thermodynamics

3.   The Law of Cause and Effect

4.   The Law of Biogenesis

5.   The Law of Gravity

Theory: In contrast to a law, a scientific theory is used to explain an observation or a set of observations. It is generally accepted to be true, though no real proof exists. The important thing about a scientific theory is that there are no experimental observations to prove it NOT true, and each piece of evidence that exists supports the theory as written. Theories are often accepted at face value since they are often difficult to prove and can be rewritten in order to include the results of all experimental observations. An example of a theory is the big bang theory. While there is no experiment that can directly test whether or not the big bang actually occurred, there is no strong evidence indicating otherwise.

Theories provide a framework to explain the **known** information of the time, but are subject to constant evaluation and updating. There is always the possibility that new evidence will conflict with a current theory.

Some examples of theories that have been rejected because they are now better explained by current knowledge:

Theory of Spontaneous Generation
Inheritance of Acquired Characteristics
The Blending Hypothesis

Some examples of theories that were initially rejected because they fell outside of the accepted knowledge of the time, but are well-accepted today due to increased knowledge and data include:

The sun-centered solar system
Warm-bloodedness in dinosaurs
The germ theory of disease
Continental drift

Hypothesis: A hypothesis is a tentative assumption made in order to draw out and test its logical or empirical consequences. Many refer to a hypothesis as an educated guess about what will happen during an experiment. A hypothesis can be based on prior knowledge and prior observations. It will be proved true or false only through experimentation.

Scientific Method: The scientific method consists of principles and procedures for the systematic pursuit of knowledge involving the recognition and formulation of a problem, the collection of data through observation and experiment, and the formulation and testing of hypotheses. The steps in the scientific method can be found elsewhere in this text.

While an inquiry may start at any point in this method and may not involve all of the steps here is the pattern.

Observations
Scientific questions result from observations of events in nature or events observed in the laboratory. An **observation** is not just a look at what happens. It also includes measurements and careful records of the event. Records could include photos, drawings, or written descriptions. The observations and data collection lead to a question. In physics, observations almost always deal with the behavior of matter. Having arrived at a question, a scientist usually researches the scientific literature to see what is known about the question. Maybe the question has already been answered. The scientist then may want to test the answer found in the literature. Or, maybe the research will lead to a new question.

Sometimes the same observations are made over and over again and are always the same. For example, you can observe that daylight lasts longer in summer than in winter. This observation never varies. Such observations are called **laws** of nature. One of the most important scientific laws was discovered in the late 1700s. Chemists observed that no mass was ever lost or gained in chemical reactions. This law became known as the law of conservation of mass. Explaining this law was a major topic of scientific research in the early 19th century.

Hypothesis

If the question has not been answered, the scientist may prepare for an experiment by making a hypothesis. A **hypothesis** is a statement of a possible answer to the question. It is a tentative explanation for a set of facts and can be tested by experiments. Although hypotheses are usually based on observations, they may also be based on a sudden idea or intuition.

Experiment

An **experiment** tests the hypothesis to determine whether it may be a correct answer to the question or a solution to the problem. Some experiments may test the effect of one thing on another under controlled conditions. Such experiments have two variables. The experimenter controls one variable, callred the *independent variable*. The other variable, the *dependent variable*, is the change caused by changing the independent variable.

For example, suppose a researcher wanted to test the effect of vitamin A on the ability of rats to see in dim light. The independent variable would be the dose of Vitamin A added to the rats' diet. The dependent variable would be the intensity of light that causes the rats to react. All other factors, such as time, temperature, age, water given to the rats, the other nutrients given to the rats, and similar factors, are held constant. Scientists sometimes do short experiments "just to see what happens". Often, these are not formal experiments. Rather they are ways of making additional observations about the behavior of matter.

In most experiments, scientists collect quantitative data, which is data that can be measured with instruments. They also collect qualitative data, descriptive information from observations other than measurements. Interpreting data and analyzing observations are important. If data is not organized in a logical manner, wrong conclusions can be drawn. Also, other scientists may not be able to follow your work or repeat your results.

Conclusion

Finally, a scientist must draw conclusions from the experiment. A conclusion must address the hypothesis on which the experiment was based. The conclusion states whether or not the data supports the hypothesis. If it does not, the conclusion should state what the experiment *did* show. If the hypothesis is not supported, the scientist uses the observations from the experiment to make a new or revised hypothesis. Then, new experiments are planned.

Theory

When a hypothesis survives many experimental tests to determine its validity, the hypothesis may evolve into a **theory**. A theory explains a body of facts and laws that are based on the facts. A theory also reliably predicts the outcome of related events in nature. For example, the law of conservation of matter and many other experimental observations led to a theory proposed early in the 19th century. This theory explained the conservation law by proposing that all matter is made up of atoms which are never created or destroyed in chemical reactions, only rearranged. This atomic theory also successfully predicted the behavior of matter in chemical reactions that had not been studied at the time. As a result, the atomic theory has stood for 200 years with only small modifications.

A theory also serves as a scientific **model**. A model can be a physical model made of wood or plastic, a computer program that simulates events in nature, or simply a mental picture of an idea. A model illustrates a theory and explains nature. For instance, in your science class you may develop a mental (and maybe a physical) model of the atom and its behavior. Outside of science, the word theory is often used to describe someone's unproven notion about something. In science, theory means much more. It is a thoroughly tested explanation of things and events observed in nature.

A theory can never be proven true, but it can be proven untrue. All it takes to prove a theory untrue is to show an exception to the theory. The test of the hypothesis may be observations of phenomena or a model may be built to examine its behavior under certain circumstances.

Steps of a Scientific Method

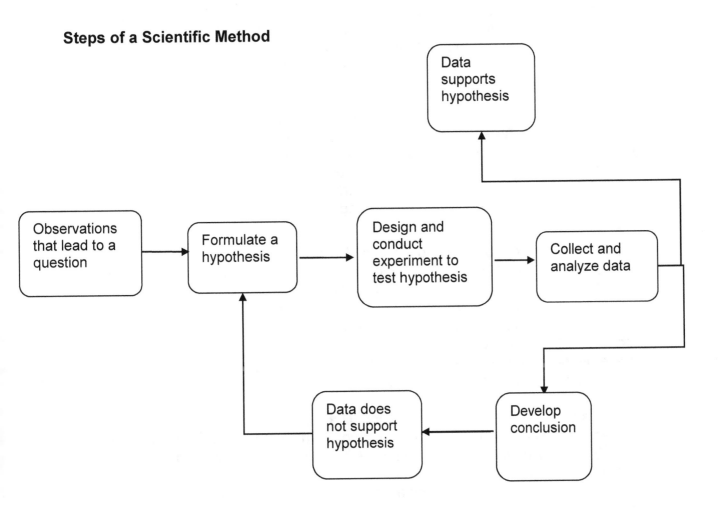

A scientific model is a set of ideas that describes a natural process and are developed by empirical or theoretical methods. They help scientists focus on the basic fundamental processes. They may be physical representations, such as a space-filling model of a molecule or a map, or they may be mathematical algorithms.

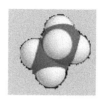

Whatever form they take, scientific models are based on what is known about the systems or objects at the time that the models are constructed. Models usually evolve and are improved as scientific advances are made. Sometimes a model must be discarded because new findings show it to be misleading or incorrect.

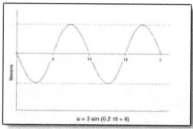

Models are developed in an effort to explain how things work in nature. Because models are not the "real thing", they can never correctly represent the system or object in all respects. The amount of detail that they contain depends upon how the model will be used as well as the sophistication and skill of the scientist doing the modeling. If a model has too many details left out, its usefulness may be limited. But too many details may make a model too complicated to be useful. So it is easy to see why models lack some features of the real system.

To overcome this difficulty, different models are often used to describe the same system or object. Scientists must then choose which model most closely fits the scientific investigation being carried out, which includes findings that are being described, and, in some cases, which one is compatible with the sophistication of the investigation itself. For example, there are many models of atoms. The solar system model described above is adequate for some purposes because electrons have properties of matter. They have mass and charge and they are found in motion in the space outside the nucleus. However, a highly mathematical model based on the field of quantum mechanics is necessary when describing the energy (or wave) properties of electrons in the atom.

Scientific models are based on physical observations that establish some facts about the system or object of interest. Scientists then combine these facts with appropriate laws or scientific principles and assumptions to produce a "picture" that mimics the behavior of the system or object to the greatest possible extent. It is on the basis of such models that science makes many of its most important advances because models provide a vehicle for making predictions about the behavior of a system or object. The predictions can then be tested as new measurements, technology or theories are applied to the subject. The new information may result in modification and refinement of the model, although certain issues may remain unresolved by the model for years. The goal, however, is to continue to develop the model in such a way as to move it ever closer to a true description of the natural phenomenon. In this way, models are vital to the scientific process.

Skill 1.2 Identify potentially hazardous situations in a physics laboratory and classroom, methods or prevention, and corrective actions.

Safety is a learned behavior and must be incorporated into instructional plans. Measures of prevention and procedures for dealing with emergencies in hazardous situations have to be in place and readily available for reference. Copies of these must be given to all people concerned, such as administrators and students.

The single most important aspect of safety is planning and anticipating various possibilities and preparing for the eventuality. Any Physics teacher/educator planning on doing an experiment must try it before the students do it. In the event of an emergency, quick action can prevent many disasters. The teacher/educator must be willing to seek help at once without any hesitation because sometimes it may not be clear that the situation is hazardous and potentially dangerous.

There are a number of procedures to prevent and correct any hazardous situation. There are several safety aids available commercially such as posters, safety contracts, safety tests, safety citations, texts on safety in secondary classroom/laboratories, hand books on safety and a host of other equipment. Another important thing is to check the laboratory and classroom for safety and report it to the administrators before staring activities/experiments. We will discuss below areas that need special attention to safety.

1. Electricity: Safety in this area starts with locating the main cut off switch. All the power points, switches, and electrical connections must be checked one by one. Batteries and live wires must be checked. All checking must be done with the power turned off. The last act of assembling is to insert the plug and the first act of disassembling is to take off the plug.

2. Motion and forces: All stationary devices must be secured by C-clamps. Protective goggles must be used. Care must be taken at all times while knives, glass rods and heavy weights are used. Viewing a solar eclipse must always be indirect. When using model rockets, NASA's safety code must be implemented.

3. Heat: The master gas valve must be off at all times except while in use. Goggles and insulated gloves are to be used whenever needed. Never use closed containers for heating. Burners and gas connections must be checked periodically. Gas jets must be closed soon after the experiment is over. Fire retardant pads and quality glassware such as Pyrex must be used.

4. Pressure: While using a pressure cooker, never allow pressure to exceed 20 lb/square inch. The pressure cooker must be cooled before it is opened. Care must be taken when using mercury since it is poisonous. A drop of oil on mercury will prevent the mercury vapors from escaping.

5. Light: Broken mirrors or those with jagged edges must be discarded immediately. Sharp-edged mirrors must be taped. Spectroscopic light voltage connections must be checked periodically. Care must be taken while using ultraviolet light sources. Some students may have psychological or physiological reactions to the effects of strobe like (e.g. epilepsy).

6. Lasers: Direct exposure to lasers must not be permitted. The laser target must be made of non-reflecting material. The movement of students must be restricted during experiments with lasers. A number of precautions while using lasers must be taken – use of low power lasers, use of approved laser goggles, maintaining the room's brightness so that the pupils of the eyes remain small. Appropriate beam stops must be set up to terminate the laser beam when needed. Prisms should be set up before class to avoid unexpected reflection.

7. Sound: Fastening of the safety disc while using the high speed siren disc is very important. Teacher must be aware of the fact that sounds higher than 110 decibels will cause damage to hearing.

8. Radiation: Proper shielding must be used while doing experiments with x-rays. All tubes that are used in a physics laboratory such as vacuum tubes, heat effect tubes, magnetic or deflection tubes must be checked and used for demonstrations by the teacher. Cathode rays must be enclosed in a frame and only the teacher should move them from their storage space. Students must watch the demonstration from at least eight feet away.

9. Radioactivity: The teacher must be knowledgeable and properly trained to handle the equipment and to demonstrate. Proper shielding of radioactive material and proper handling of material are absolutely critical. Disposal of any radioactive material must comply with the guidelines of NRC.

It is important that teachers and educators follow these guidelines to protect the students and to avoid most of the hazards. They have a responsibility to protect themselves as well. **There should be not any compromises in issues of safety.**

Skill 1.3 Identify the function and use of various common physics instruments (i.e., electrical meters, oscilloscopes, signal generators, and spectrometers).

Oscilloscope: An oscilloscope is a piece of electrical test equipment that allows signal voltages to be viewed as two-dimensional graphs of electrical potential differences plotted as a function of time.

The oscilloscope functions by measuring the deflection of a beam of electrons traveling through a vacuum in a cathode ray tube. The deflection of the beam can be caused by a magnetic field outside the tube or by electrostatic energy created by plates inside the tube. The unknown voltage or potential energy difference can be determined by comparing the electron deflection it causes to the electron deflection caused by a known voltage.

Oscilloscopes can also determine if an electrical circuit is oscillating and at what frequency. They are particularly useful for troubleshooting malfunctioning equipment. You can see the "moving parts" of the circuit and tell if the signal is being distorted. With the aid of an oscilloscope you can also calculate the "noise" within a signal and see if the "noise" changes over time.

Inputs of the electrical signal are usually entered into the oscilloscope via a coaxial cable or probes. A variety of transducers can be used with an oscilloscope that enable it to measure other stimuli including sound, pressure, heat, and light.

Voltmeter/Ohmmeter/Ammeter: A common electrical meter, typically known as a multimeter, is capable of measuring voltage, resistance, and current. Many of these devices can also measure capacitance (farads), frequency (hertz), duty cycle (a percentage), temperature (degrees), conductance (siemens), and inductance (henrys).

These meters function by utilizing the following familiar equations:

Across a resistor (Resistor R):

$$V_R = IR_R$$

Across a capacitor (Capacitor C):

$$V_C = IX_C$$

Across an inductor (Inductor L):

$$V_L = IX_L$$

Where V=voltage, I=current, R=resistance, X=reactance.

If any two factors in the equations are held constant or are known, the third factor can be determined and is displayed by the multimeter.

Signal Generator: A signal generator, also known as a test signal generator, function generator, tone generator, arbitrary waveform generator, or frequency generator, is a device that generates repeating electronic signals in either the analog or digital domains. They are generally used in designing, testing, troubleshooting, and repairing electronic devices.

A function generator produces simple repetitive waveforms by utilizing a circuit called an electronic oscillator or a digital signal processor to synthesize a waveform. Common waveforms are sine, sawtooth, step or pulse, square, and triangular. Arbitrary waveform generators are also available which allow a user to create waveforms of any type within the frequency, accuracy and output limits of the generator. Function generators are typically used in simple electronics repair and design where they are used to stimulate a circuit under test. A device such as an oscilloscope is then used to measure the circuit's output.

Spectrometer: A spectrometer is an optical instrument used to measure properties of light over a portion of the electromagnetic spectrum. Light intensity is the variable that is most commonly measured but wavelength and polarization state can also be determined. A spectrometer is used in spectroscopy for producing spectral lines and measuring their wavelengths and intensities. Spectrometers are capable of operating over a wide range of wavelengths, from short wave gamma and X-rays into the far infrared. In optics, a spectrograph separates incoming light according to its wavelength and records the resulting spectrum in some detector. In astronomy, spectrographs are widely used with telescopes.

Skill 1.4   Identify leading physicists and their contributions.

Archimedes
Archimedes was a Greek mathematician, physicist, engineer, astronomer, and philosopher. He is credited with many inventions and discoveries some of which are still in use today such as the Archimedes screw. He designed the compound pulley, a system of pulleys used to lift heavy loads such as ships.

Although Archimedes did not invent the lever, he gave the first rigorous explanation of the principles involved which are the transmission of force through a fulcrum and moving the effort applied through a greater distance than the object to be moved. His Law of the Lever states that magnitudes are in equilibrium at distances reciprocally proportional to their weights.

He also laid down the laws of flotation and described Archimedes' principle which states that a body immersed in a fluid experiences a buoyant force equal to the weight of the displaced fluid.

Niels Bohr

Bohr was a Danish physicist who made fundamental contributions to understanding atomic structure and quantum mechanics. Bohr is widely considered one of the greatest physicists of the twentieth century.
Bohr's model of the atom was the first to place electrons in discrete quantized orbits around the nucleus.

Bohr also helped determine that the chemical properties of an element are largely determined by the number of electrons in the outer orbits of the atom. The idea that an electron could drop from a higher-energy orbit to a lower one emitting a photon of discrete energy originated with Bohr and became the basis for future quantum theory.

He also contributed significantly to the Copenhagen interpretation of quantum mechanics. He received the Nobel Prize for Physics for this work in 1922.

Marie Curie

Curie was as a Polish-French physicist and chemist. She was a pioneer in radioactivity and the winner of two Nobel Prizes, one in Physics and the other in Chemistry. She was also the first woman to win the Nobel Prize.

Curie studied radioactive materials, particularly pitchblende, the ore from which uranium was extracted. The ore was more radioactive than the uranium extracted from it which led the Curies (Marie and her husband Pierre) to discover a substance far more radioactive then uranium. Over several years of laboratory work the Curies eventually isolated and identified two new radioactive chemical elements, polonium and radium. Curie refined the radium isolation process and continued intensive study of the nature of radioactivity.

Albert Einstein

Einstein was a German-born theoretical physicist who is widely considered one of the greatest physicists of all time. While best known for the theory of relativity, and specifically mass-energy equivalence, $E = mc^2$, he was awarded the 1921 Nobel Prize in Physics for his explanation of the photoelectric effect and "for his services to Theoretical Physics". In his paper on the photoelectric effect, Einstein extended Planck's hypothesis ($E = h\nu$) of discrete energy elements to his own hypothesis that electromagnetic energy is absorbed or emitted by matter in quanta and proposed a new law $E_{max} = h\nu - P$ to account for the photoelectric effect.

He was known for many scientific investigations including the special theory of relativity which stemmed from an attempt to reconcile the laws of mechanics with the laws of the electromagnetic field. His general theory of relativity considered all observers to be equivalent, not only those moving at a uniform speed. In general relativity, gravity is no longer a force, as it is in Newton's law of gravity, but is a consequence of the curvature of space-time.

Other areas of physics in which Einstein made significant contributions, achievements or breakthroughs include relativistic cosmology, capillary action, critical opalescence, classical problems of statistical mechanics and problems in which they were merged with quantum theory (leading to an explanation of the Brownian movement of molecules), atomic transition probabilities, the quantum theory of a monatomic gas, the concept of the photon, the theory of radiation (including stimulated emission), and the geometrization of physics.

Einstein's research efforts after developing the theory of general relativity consisted primarily of attempts to generalize his theory of gravitation in order to unify and simplify the fundamental laws of physics, particularly gravitation and electromagnetism, which he referred to as the Unified Field Theory.

Michael Faraday

Faraday was an English chemist and physicist who contributed significantly to the fields of electromagnetism and electrochemistry. He established that magnetism could affect rays of light and that the two phenomena were linked. It was largely due to his efforts that electricity became viable for use in technology. The unit for capacitance, the farad, is named after him as is the Faraday constant, the charge on a mole of electrons (about 96,485 coulombs). Faraday's law of induction states that a magnetic field changing in time creates a proportional electromotive force.

J. Robert Oppenheimer

Oppenheimer was an American physicist, best known for his role as the scientific director of the Manhattan Project, the effort to develop the first nuclear weapons. Sometimes called "the father of the atomic bomb", Oppenheimer later lamented the use of atomic weapons. He became a chief advisor to the United States Atomic Energy Commission and lobbied for international control of atomic energy. Oppenheimer was one of the founders of the American school of theoretical physics at the University of California, Berkeley. He did important research in theoretical astrophysics, nuclear physics, spectroscopy, and quantum field theory.

Sir Isaac Newton

Newton was an English physicist, mathematician, astronomer, alchemist, and natural philosopher in the late 17th and early 18th centuries. He described universal gravitation and the three laws of motion laying the groundwork for classical mechanics. He was the first to show that the motion of objects on earth and in space is governed by the same set of mechanical laws. These laws became central to the scientific revolution that took place during this period of history. Newton's three laws of motion are:

I. Every object in a state of uniform motion tends to remain in that state of motion unless an external force is applied to it.

II. The relationship between an object's mass m, its acceleration a, and the applied force F is F = ma.

III. For every action there is an equal and opposite reaction.

In mechanics, Newton developed the basic principles of conservation of momentum. In optics, he invented the reflecting telescope and discovered that the spectrum of colors seen when white light passes through a prism is inherent in the white light and not added by the prism as previous scientists had claimed. Newton notably argued that light is composed of particles. He also formulated an experimental law of cooling, studied the speed of sound, and proposed a theory of the origin of stars.

Skill 1.5 Distinguish between the four fundamental forces of nature in terms of the particles they act upon, relative distances over which they act, and their relative strengths.

There are four fundamental forces that control the behavior of all matter and describe all physical phenomena; gravity, weak interaction, electromagnetism, and strong interaction. Amazingly these same forces control the tiniest sub-nuclear particles, all the life forms on Earth, and the movement of all the planets in the universe. Most physicists believe that we will ultimately be able to understand even these forces as one single, fundamental interaction. Electricity and magnetism were once thought to be separate forces, but we now know that they are parts of a single theory of electromagnetism. Electroweak theory has helped to tie weak interactions with electromagnetism. Likewise, we may eventually combine all four fundamental forces into a single relationship. Note that, while they are called forces, these interactions are not forces in the classic Newtonian sense.

The four forces interact on largely different scales and using different mediators, as will be shown below. They are listed from weakest to strongest; if we assigned gravity a relative strength of 1, then the weak interaction would be 10^{25} times stronger, the electromagnetic by a factor of 10^{36}, and the strong interaction by a factor of 10^{38}.

Gravity: Though gravity is the weakest interaction, it has infinite range and affects all masses. Thus, it is responsible for the structure of galaxies, the orbits of planets, and the expansion of the universe as well as everyday phenomena such as the falling of objects. Gravity is mediated by elementary particles known as gravitons and is currently understood through the theory of General Relativity.

Weak interaction: Despite the name, weak interactions are much stronger than gravity but with a much smaller range. They are responsible for certain phenomena occurring in the atomic nucleus, including beta decay, and other occurrences on this size scale. Weak interactions are mediated by bosons and understood through the Electroweak Theory.

Electromagnetism: This force acts on charged particles and, like gravity, has a large enough range that we can observe its effect in everyday occurrences. Electromagnetism is responsible for a wide range of phenomena ranging from rainbows and sound to lasers and the structure of metal. It is mediate by photons and understood through the theory of Quantum Electrodynamics (QED).

Strong interactions: Strong interactions work primarily on sub-atomic particles though their range is theoretically infinite. They are responsible for holding protons and neutrons together. Nuclear force, which holds the nucleus together, is a byproduct of strong interactions. This demonstrates the large strength of these interactions, since electromagnetic forces would otherwise cause the protons in the nucleus to repel one another. Strong interactions are mediated by gluons and understood through the theory of Quantum Chromodynamics.

COMPETENCY II.   KNOWLEDGE OF THE MATHEMATICS OF PHYSICS

Skill 2.1 Determine if a formula could be valid based on dimensional analysis.

Dimensional analysis is simply a technique in which the units of the variables in an equation are analyzed. It is often used by scientists and engineers to determine if a derived equation or computation is plausible. While it does not guarantee that a stated relationship is correct, it does tell us that the relationship is at least reasonable. When there is a mix of various physical quantities being equated in a relationship, the units of both sides of the equation must be the same. We will examine a simple example to demonstrate how dimensional analysis can be used:

The Ideal Gas Law is used to predict change in temperature, volume, or pressure of a gas. It is:

$$PV = nRT$$

Where P=pressure [Pa]
V=volume [m³]
n=numbers of moles of gas [mol]
T=temperature [K]
R=the gas constant 8.314472 [m³·Pa·K⁻¹·mol⁻¹]

Show that this formula is physically plausible using dimensional analysis.

Begin by substituting the units of each quantity into the equation:

$$[Pa] \times [m^3] = [mol] \left[\frac{[m^3] \times [Pa]}{[K] \times [mol]} \right] [K]$$

On the right-hand side of the equation, we can cancel [mol] and [K]:

$$[Pa] \times [m^3] = [m^3] \times [Pa]$$

Because this is a simple example, we can already see that the two sides of the equations have the same units. In more complicated equations, additional manipulation may be required to elucidate this fact. Now, we can confidently believe in the plausibility of this relationship.

Skill 2.2 Combine vectors using graphic and trigonometric methods.

Vector space is a collection of objects that have magnitude and direction. They may have mathematical operations, such as addition, subtraction, and scaling, applied to them. Vectors are usually displayed in boldface or with an arrow above the letter. They are usually shown in graphs or other diagrams as arrows. The length of the arrow represents the magnitude of the vector while the direction in which it points shows the direction.

To add two vectors graphically, the base of the second vector is drawn from the point of the first vector as shown below with vectors **A** and **B**. The sum of the vectors is drawn as a dashed line, from the base of the first vector to the tip of the second. As illustrated, the order in which the vectors are connected is not significant as the endpoint is the same graphically whether **A** connects to **B** or **B** connects to **A**. This principle is sometimes called the parallelogram rule.

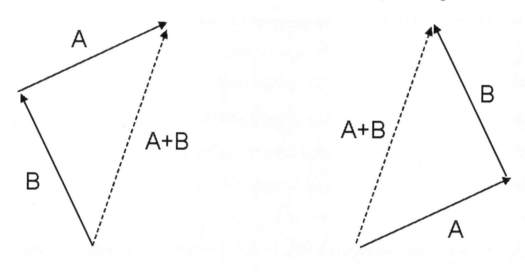

If more than two vectors are to be combined, additional vectors are simply drawn in accordingly with the sum vector connecting the base of the first to the tip of the final vector.

Subtraction of two vectors can be geometrically defined as follows. To subtract **A** from **B**, place the ends of **A** and **B** at the same point and then draw an arrow from the tip of **A** to the tip of **B**. That arrow represents the vector **B-A**, as illustrated below:

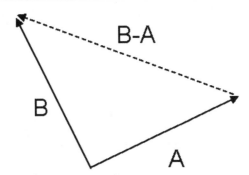

To add two vectors without drawing them, the vectors must be broken down into their orthogonal components using sine, cosine, and tangent functions. Add both x components to get the total x component of the sum vector, then add both y components to get the y component of the sum vector. Use the Pythagorean Theorem and the three trigonometric functions to the get the size and direction of the final vector.

<u>Example</u>: Here is a diagram showing the x and y-components of a vector D1:

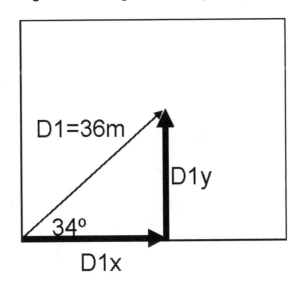

Notice that the x-component D1x is adjacent to the angle of 34 degrees.

Thus D1x=36m (cos34) =29.8m

The y-component is opposite to the angle of 34 degrees.

Thus D1y =36m (sin34) = 20.1m

A second vector D2 is broken up into its components in the diagram below using the same techniques. We find that D2y=9.0m and D2x=-18.5m.

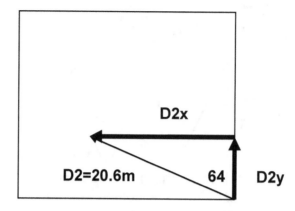

Next we add the x components and the y components to get

DTotal x =11.3 m   *and*   DTotal y =29.1 m

Now we have to use the Pythagorean theorem to get the total magnitude of the final vector. And the arctangent function to find the direction. As shown in the diagram below.

DTotal=31.2m

tan θ= DTotal y / DTotal x = 29.1m / 11.3 =2.6   θ=69 degrees

Skill 2.3   Determine the dot product and cross product of two vectors.

The dot product is also known as the scalar product. This is because the dot product of two vectors is not a vector, but a scalar (i.e., a real number without an associated direction). The definition of the dot product of the two vectors **a** and **b** is:

$$a \bullet b = \sum_{i=1}^{n} a_i b_i = a_1 b_1 + a_2 b_2 + ... + a_n b_n$$

The following is an example calculation of the dot product of two vectors:

$$[1\ 3\ -5] \cdot [4\ -2\ -2] = (1)(4) + (3)(-2) + (-5)(-2) = 8$$

Note that the product is a simple scalar quantity, not a vector. The dot product is commutative and distributive.

Unlike the dot product, the cross product does return another vector. The vector returned by the cross product is orthogonal to the two original vectors. The cross product is defined as:

$$\mathbf{a} \times \mathbf{b} = n\,|\mathbf{a}|\,|\mathbf{b}|\sin\theta$$

where n is a unit vector perpendicular to both **a** and **b** and θ is the angle between **a** and **b**. In practice, the cross product can be calculated as explained below:

Given the orthogonal unit vectors **i**, **,j**, and **k**, the vector **a** and **b** can be expressed:

$$\mathbf{a} = a_1\mathbf{i} + a_2\mathbf{j} + a_3\mathbf{k}$$
$$\mathbf{b} = b_1\mathbf{i} + b_2\mathbf{j} + b_3\mathbf{k}$$

Then we can calculate that

$$\mathbf{a} \times \mathbf{b} = \mathbf{i}(a_2b_3)+\mathbf{j}(a_3b_1)+\mathbf{k}(a_1b_2)-\mathbf{i}(a_3b_2)-\mathbf{j}(a_1b_3)-\mathbf{k}(a_2b_1)$$

The cross product is anticommutative (that is, $\mathbf{a} \times \mathbf{b} = -\mathbf{b} \times \mathbf{a}$) and distributive over addition.

Skill 2.4 Report the answer of a given calculation according to the rules of significant figures.

Significant figures are important to denote the degree of certainty we can have in a given measurement or calculation. Rules exist to allow us to first calculate the number of significant figures in a given quantity and then to determine how many significant figures should remain following an operation. First, how to determine the number of significant figures in a quantity:

1. Non-zero digits are always significant.
2. Any zeros between two significant digits are significant.
3. A final zero or trailing zeros in the decimal portion <u>ONLY</u> are significant.

For instance, the number of significant figures in the following measurements are as follows:

1) 3.0800   5 significant figures

2) 0.00418   3 significant figures

3) 7.09×10^{-5} 3 significant figures

4) 91,600   3 significant figures

Now the rules for operations:

1. For multiplication or division, keep the same number of significant figures as the factor with the *fewest* significant figures.

2. For addition or subtraction, keep the same number of decimal places as the term with the *fewest*.

Here are examples of each of these rules:

1) 1.2 x 4.56 = 5.472 but since the first factor has only 2 significant figures, the answer must be also have 2 significant figures and is 5.5
2) 1.234 + 5.67 = 6.904 but since the second term has only 2 decimal places, so must the answer which is 6.90

Skill 2.5 Determine the propagation of error based on uncertainty in measurement.

Often in scientific operations we want to determine a quantity that requires many steps to measure. Of course, each time we take a measurement there will be a certain associated error that is a function of the measuring device. Each of these errors contributes to an even greater one in the final value. This phenomenon is known as propagation of error or propagation of uncertainty.

A measured value is typically expressed in the form $x \pm \Delta x$, where Δx is the uncertainty or margin of error. What this means is that the value of the measured quantity lies somewhere between $x - \Delta x$ and $x + \Delta x$, but our measurement techniques do not allow us any more precision. If several measurements are required to ultimately decide a value, we must use formulas to determine the total uncertainty that results from all the measurement errors. A few of these formulas for simple functions are listed below:

Formula	Uncertainty
$X = A \pm B$	$(\Delta X)^2 = (\Delta A)^2 + (\Delta B)^2$
$X = cA$	$\Delta X = c \Delta A$
$X = c(A \cdot B)$	$\left(\dfrac{\Delta X}{X}\right)^2 = \left(\dfrac{\Delta A}{A}\right)^2 + \left(\dfrac{\Delta B}{B}\right)^2$
$X = c\left(\dfrac{A}{B}\right)$	$\left(\dfrac{\Delta X}{X}\right)^2 = \left(\dfrac{\Delta A}{A}\right)^2 + \left(\dfrac{\Delta B}{B}\right)^2$

For example, if we wanted to determine the density of a small piece of metal we would have to measure its weight on a scale and then determine its volume by measuring the amount of water it displaces in a graduated cylinder. There will be error associated with measurements made by both the scale and the graduated cylinder. Let's suppose we took the following measurements:

Mass: 57± 0.5 grams
Volume: 23 ± 3 mm^3

Since density is simply mass divided by the volume, we can determine its value to be:

$$\rho = \frac{m}{V} = \frac{57g}{23mm^3} = 2.5\frac{g}{mm^3}$$

Now we must calculate the uncertainty on this measurement, using the formula above:

$$\left(\frac{\Delta x}{x}\right)^2 = \left(\frac{\Delta A}{A}\right)^2 + \left(\frac{\Delta B}{B}\right)^2$$

$$\Delta x = \left(\sqrt{\left(\frac{\Delta A}{A}\right)^2 + \left(\frac{\Delta B}{B}\right)^2}\right)x = \left(\sqrt{\left(\frac{0.5g}{57g}\right)^2 + \left(\frac{3mm^3}{23mm^3}\right)^2}\right) \times 2.5\frac{g}{mm^3} = 0.3\frac{g}{mm^3}$$

Thus, the final value for the density of this object is 2.5 ± 0.3 g/mm^3.

Skill 2.6 Identify the precision of a given measuring device.

Precision is basically a measure of how similar repeated measurements from a given device or technique are. Note that this is distinguished from accuracy which refers to how close to "correct" a measuring device or technique is. Thus, accuracy can be tested by measuring a known quantity (a standard) and determining how close the value provided by the measuring device is. To determine precision, however, we must make multiple measurements of the same sample.

The precision of an instrument is typically given in terms of its standard error or standard deviation. Precision is typically divided into reproducibility and repeatability. These concepts are subtly different and are defined as follows:

Repeatability: Variation observed in measurements made over a short period of time while trying to keep all conditions the same (including using the same instrument, the same environmental conditions, and the same operator)

Reproducibility: Variation observed in measurements taken over a long time period in a variety of different settings (different places and environments, using different instruments and operators)

Both repeatability and reproducibility can be estimated by taking multiple measurements under the conditions specified above. Using the obtained values, standard deviation can be calculated using the formula:

$$\sigma = \sqrt{\frac{1}{N}\sum_{i=1}^{N}(x_i - \overline{x})^2}$$

where σ = standard deviation
$\quad$ N = the number of measurements
$\quad$ x_i = the individual measured values
$\quad$ $\overline{x}$ = the average value of the measured quantity

To obtain a reliable estimate of standard deviation, N, the number of samples, should be fairly large. We can use statistical methods to determine a confidence interval on our measurements. A typical confidence level for scientific investigations is 90% or 95%.

Skill 2.7 Convert between dimensional units.

Examples of conversion are given below in Section II-8.

Skill 2.8 Identify prefixes in the metric system and standard units of measure (e.g., Newtons, meters, kilowatt hours, tesla, electron volts, calories, horsepower).

SI is an abbreviation of the French *Système International d'Unités* or the **International System of Units**. It is the most widely used system of units in the world and is the system used in science. The use of many SI units in the United States is increasing outside of science and technology. There are two types of SI units: **base units** and **derived units**. The base units are:

Quantity	Unit name	Symbol
Length	meter	m
Mass	kilogram	kg
Amount of substance	mole	mol
Time	second	s
Temperature	kelvin	K
Electric current	ampere	A
Luminous intensity	candela	cd

The name "kilogram" occurs for the SI base unit of mass for historical reasons. Derived units are formed from the kilogram, but appropriate decimal prefixes are attached to the word "gram." Derived units measure a quantity that may be **expressed in terms of other units**. Some derived units important for physics are:

Derived quantity	Unit name	Expression in terms of other units	Symbol
Area	square meter	m^2	
Volume	cubic meter liter	m^3 $dm^3 = 10^{-3}\ m^3$	 L or l
Mass	unified atomic mass unit	$(6.022 \times 10^{23})^{-1}\ g$	u or Da
Time	minute hour day	60 s 60 min = 3600 s 24 h = 86400 s	min h d
Speed	meter per second	m/s	
Acceleration	meter per second squared	m/s^2	
Temperature*	degree Celsius	K	°C
Mass density	gram per liter	$g/L = 1\ kg/m^3$	
Force	newton	$m \cdot kg/s^2$	N
Pressure	pascal standard atmosphere§	$N/m^2 = kg/(m \cdot s^2)$ 101325 Pa	Pa atm
Energy, Work, Heat	joule nutritional calorie§	$N \cdot m = m^3 \cdot Pa = m^2 \cdot kg/s^2$ 4184 J	J Cal
Heat (molar)	joule per mole	J/mol	
Heat capacity, entropy	joule per kelvin	J/K	
Heat capacity (molar), entropy (molar)	joule per mole kelvin	$J/(mol \cdot K)$	
Specific heat	joule per kilogram kelvin	$J/(kg \cdot K)$	
Power	watt	J/s	W
Electric charge	coulomb	$s \cdot A$	C
Electric potential, electromotive force	volt	W/A	V
Viscosity	pascal second	$Pa \cdot s$	
Surface tension	newton per meter	N/m	

*Temperature differences in Kelvin are the same as those differences in degrees Celsius. To obtain degrees Celsius from Kelvin, subtract 273.15. Differentiate *m* and meters (m) by context.
§These are commonly used non-SI units.

Decimal multiples of SI units are formed by attaching a **prefix** directly before the unit and a symbol prefix directly before the unit symbol. SI prefixes range from 10^{-24} to 10^{24}. Common prefixes you are likely to encounter in physics are shown below:

Factor	Prefix	Symbol	Factor	Prefix	Symbol
10^9	*giga—*	G	10^{-1}	*deci—*	d
10^6	*mega—*	M	10^{-2}	*centi—*	c
10^3	*kilo—*	k	10^{-3}	*milli—*	m
10^2	*hecto—*	h	10^{-6}	*micro—*	μ
10^1	*deca—*	da	10^{-9}	*nano—*	n
			10^{-12}	*pico—*	p

Example: 0.0000004355 meters is 4.355×10^{-7} m or 435.5×10^{-9} m. This length is also 435.5 nm or 435.5 nanometers.

Example: Find a unit to express the volume of a cubic crystal that is 0.2 mm on each side so that the number before the unit is between 1 and 1000.

Solution: Volume is length X width X height, so this volume is $(0.0002 \text{ m})^3$ or 8×10^{-12} m³. Conversions of volumes and areas using powers of units of length must take the power into account. Therefore:
$$1 \text{ m}^3 = 10^3 \text{ dm}^3 = 10^6 \text{ cm}^3 = 10^9 \text{ mm}^3 = 10^{18} \text{ } \mu\text{m}^3,$$
The length 0.0002 m is 2×10^2 μm, so the volume is also 8×10^6 μm³. This volume could also be expressed as 8×10^{-3} mm³. None of these numbers, however, is between 1 and 1000.

Expressing volume in liters is helpful in cases like these. There is no power on the unit of liters, therefore:
$$1 \text{ L} = 10^3 \text{ mL} = 10^6 \text{ } \mu\text{L} = 10^9 \text{ nL}.$$
Converting cubic meters to liters gives
$$8 \times 10^{-12} \text{ m}^3 \times \frac{10^3 \text{ L}}{1 \text{ m}^3} = 8 \times 10^{-9} \text{ L}. \text{ The crystal's volume is 8 nanoliters}$$
(8 nL).

Example: Determine the ideal gas constant, R, in L•atm/(mol•K) from its SI value of 8.3144 J/(mol•K).

Solution: One joule is identical to one m³•Pa (see the table on the previous page).
$$8.3144 \frac{\text{m}^3 \bullet \text{Pa}}{\text{mol} \bullet \text{K}} \times \frac{1000 \text{ L}}{1 \text{ m}^3} \times \frac{1 \text{ atm}}{101325 \text{ Pa}} = 0.082057 \frac{\text{L} \bullet \text{atm}}{\text{mol} \bullet \text{K}}$$

Skill 2.9 Determine the order of magnitude of a physical quantity, based upon reasonable estimation.

The order of magnitude refers to a category of scale or size of an amount, where each category contains values of a fixed ratio to the categories before or after. The most common ratio is 10. The table to the left lists the orders of magnitude of the number 10 associated with the actual numbers.

Powers of ten	Order of magnitude
0.0001	−4
0.001	−3
0.01	−2
0.1	−1
1	0
10	1
100	2
1,000	3
10,000	4

Orders of magnitude are typically used to make estimations of a number. For example, if two numbers differ by one order of magnitude, one number is 10 times larger than the other. If they differ by two orders of magnitude the difference is 100 times larger or smaller, and so on. It follows that two numbers have the same order of magnitude if they differ by less than 10 times the size.

To estimate the order of manitude of a physical quantity, you round the its value to the nearest power of 10. For example, in estimating the human population of the earth, you may not know if it is 5 billion or 12 billion, but a reasonable order of magnitude estimate is 10 billion. Similarly, you may know that Saturn is much larger than Earth and can estiamte that it has approximatly 100 times more mass, or that its mass is 2 orders of magnitude larger. The actual number is 95 times the mass of earth.

Physical Item	Size	Order of Magnitude (meters)
Diameter of a hydrogen atom	100 picometers	10^{-10}
Size of a bacteria	1 micrometer	10^{-6}
Size of a raindrop	1 millimeter	10^{-3}
Width of a human finger	1 centimeter	10^{-2}
Height of Washinton Monument	100 meters	10^{2}
Height of Mount Everest	10 kilometers	10^{4}
Diameter of Earth	10 million meters	10^{7}
One light year	1 light year	10^{16}

Skill 2.10 Analyze the slope of a graph in specific regions either curved or linear, including units.

The slope or the gradient of a line is used to describe the measurement of the steepness, incline, or grade. A higher slope value indicates a steeper incline. The slope is defined as the ratio of the "rise" divided by the "run" between two points on a line, that is to say, the ratio of the altitude change to the horizontal distance between any two points on the line.

The slope of a line in the plane containing the x and y axes is generally represented by the letter m, and is defined as the change in the y coordinate divided by the corresponding change in the x coordinate, between two distinct points on the line. This is described by the following equation:

$$m = \frac{\Delta y}{\Delta x}$$

Given two points (x1, y1) and (x2, y2), the change in x from one to the other is x2 - x1, while the change in y is y2 - y1. Substituting both quantities into the above equation obtains the following:

$$m = \frac{y_2 - y_1}{x_2 - x_1}$$

For example: if a line runs through two points: P(1,2) and Q(13,8). By dividing the difference in y-coordinates by the difference in x-coordinates, one can obtain the slope of the line:

$$m = \frac{\Delta y}{\Delta x} = \frac{y_2 - y_1}{x_2 - x_1} = \frac{8 - 2}{13 - 1} = \frac{6}{12} = \frac{1}{2}$$

The slope is 1/2 = 0.5.

The slope of curved lines can be approximated by selecting x and y values that are very close together. In a curved region the slope changes along the curve.

If we let Δx and Δy be the x and y distances between two points on a curve, then $\Delta y / \Delta x$ is the slope of a secant line to the curve.

For example, the slope of the secant intersecting
y = x² at (0,0) and (3,9)
is m = (9 - 0) / (3 - 0) = 3

By moving the two points closer together so that Δy and Δx decrease, the secant line more closely approximates a tangent line to the curve, and as such the slope of the secant approaches that of the tangent.

In differential calculus, the derivative is essentially taking the change in y with respect to the change in x as the change in x approaches the limit of zero. The derivative of the curved line function is a line tangent to that point on the curve and is equal to the slope of the graph at that specific point.

Skill 2.11 Analyze the area under a graph in specific regions either curved or linear, including units.

In calculus, the integral of a function is an extension of the concept of summing and is given by the area under a graphical representation of the function. The integral is usually used to find a measure of totality such as area, volume, mass, or displacement when the rate of change is specified, as in any simple x-y graphical representation.

The simplest graph to analyze the area under is a flat horizontal line. As an example, let's say f is the constant function $f(x) = 3$ and we want to find the area under the graph from x= 0 to x=10. This is simply a rectangle 3 units high by 10 units long, or 30 units square. The same result can be found by integrating the function, though this is usually done for more complicated or smooth curves.

Let us imagine the curve of a function f(X) between X=0 and X=10. One way to approximate the area under the curve is to draw numerous rectangles under the curve of a given width, estimate their height and sum the area of each rectangle. We can say that the width of each rectangle is δX. But since the top of each column is not exactly straight, this is only an approximation.

When we use integral calculus to determine an integral, we are taking the limit of δX approaching zero, so there will be more and more columns which are thinner and thinner to fill the space between X=0 and X=10. The top of each column then gets closer and closer to being a straight line and our expression for the area therefore gets closer and closer to being exactly right.

Skill 2.12   Convert temperature in one scale given temperature in another scale.

There are four generally recognized temperature scales, Celsius, Fahrenheit, Kelvin and Rankine. The Kelvin and Rankine scales are absolute temperature scales corresponding to the Celsius and Fahrenheit scales, respectively. Absolute temperature scales have a zero reading when the temperature reaches absolute zero (the theoretical point at which no thermal energy exists). The absolute temperature scales are useful for many calculations in chemistry and physics.

To convert between Celsius and Fahrenheit, use the following relationship:
$$x \, °F = (5/9)(x - 32) \, °C$$
To convert to the absolute temperature scales, use the appropriate conversion below:
$$x \, °F = x + 459.67 \, °R$$
$$x \, °C = x + 273.15 \, K$$
Note that the size of each degree on the Fahrenheit/ Rankine scale is smaller than the size of a degree on the Celsius/Kelvin scale.

COMPETENCY III.   KNOWLEDGE OF THERMODYNAMICS

Skill 3.1   Solve and analyze the change in length, area, or volume due to temperature change.

Most materials expand when heated with a change in dimension proportional to the change in temperature. A notable exception to this is water between 0^0C and 4^0C.

If we consider a long rod of length L that increases in length by ΔL when heated, the fractional change in length $\Delta L / L$ is directly proportional to the change in temperature ΔT.

$$\Delta L / L = \alpha.\Delta T$$

The constant of proportionality α is known as the **coefficient of linear expansion** and is a property of the material of which the rod is made.

Problem: The temperature of an iron rod 10 meters long changes from -3^0C to 12^0C. If iron has a coefficient of linear expansion of 0.000011 per ^0C, by how much does the rod expand?

Solution: The length of the rod L = 10 meters.
Change in temperature $\Delta T = 12^0C - (-3^0C) = 15^0C$
Change in length of the rod $\Delta L = 0.000011 \times 10 \times 15 = .00165$ meters

If instead of a rod, we consider an area A that increases by ΔA when heated, we find that the fractional change in area is proportional to the change in temperature ΔT. The proportionality constant in this case is known as the **coefficient of area expansion** and is related to the coefficient of linear expansion as demonstrated below.

If A is a rectangle with dimensions L_1 and L_2, then

$$A + \Delta A = (L_1 + \Delta L_1)(L_2 + \Delta L_2)$$
$$= (L_1 + \alpha L_1 \Delta T)(L_2 + \alpha L_2 \Delta T)$$
$$= L_1 L_2 + 2\alpha L_1 L_2 \Delta T + \alpha^2 (\Delta T)^2$$

Ignoring the higher order term for small changes in temperature, we find that

$$\Delta A = 2\alpha A \Delta T = \gamma A \Delta T$$

Thus the coefficient of area expansion $\gamma = 2\alpha$.

Following the same procedure as above, we can show that the change in volume of a material when heated may be expressed as

$$\Delta V = 3\alpha V \Delta T = \beta V \Delta T$$

where the **coefficient of volume expansion** $\beta = 3\alpha$.

Problem: An aluminum sphere of radius 10cm is heated from $0^0 C$ to $25^0 C$. What is the change in its volume? The coefficient of linear expansion of aluminum is 0.000024 per $^0 C$.

Solution: Volume V of the sphere = $\frac{4}{3}\Pi r^3 = \frac{4}{3} \times 3.14 \times 1000 cm^3 = 4186.67 cm^3$

Change in volume of the sphere = $3 \times 0.000024 \times 4186.67 \times 25 = 7.54 cm^3$

Skill 3.2 Distinguish between the three methods of heat transfer.

All heat transfer is the movement of thermal energy from hot to cold matter. This movement down a thermal gradient is a consequence of the second law of thermodynamics. The three methods of heat transfer are listed and explained below.

Conduction: Electron diffusion or photo vibration is responsible for this mode of heat transfer. The bodies of matter themselves do not move; the heat is transferred because adjacent atoms that vibrate against each other or as electrons flow between atoms. This type of heat transfer is most common when two solids come in direct contact with each other. This is because molecules in a solid are in close contact with one another and so the electrons can flow freely. It stands to reason, then, that metals are good conductors of thermal energy. This is because their metallic bonds allow the freest movement of electrons. Similarly, conduction is better in denser solids. Examples of conduction can be seen in the use of copper to quickly convey heat in cooking pots, the flow of heat from a hot water bottle to a person's body, or the cooling of a warm drink with ice.

Convection: Convection involves some conduction but is distinct in that it involves the movement of warm particles to cooler areas. Convection may be either natural or forced, depending on how the current of warm particles develops. Natural convection occurs when molecules near a heat source absorb thermal energy (typically via conduction), become less dense, and rise. Cooler molecules then take their place and a natural current is formed. Forced convection, as the name suggests, occurs when liquids or gases are moved by pumps, fans, or other means to be brought into contact with warmer or cooler masses. Because the free motion of particles with different thermal energy is key to this mode of heat transfer, convection is most common in liquid and gases. Convection can, however, transfer heat between a liquid or gas and a solid.

Forced convection is used in "forced air" home heating systems and is common in industrial manufacturing processes. Additionally, natural convection is responsible for ocean currents and many atmospheric events. Finally, natural convection often arises in association with conduction, for instance in the air near a radiator or the water in a pot on the stove.

Radiation: This method of heat transfer occurs via electromagnetic radiation. All matter warmer than absolute zero (that is, all known matter) radiates heat. This radiation occurs regardless of the presence of any medium. Thus, it occurs even in a vacuum. Since light and radiant heat are both part of the EM spectrum, we can easily visualize how heat is transferred via radiation. For instance, just like light, radiant heat is reflected by shiny materials and absorbed by dark materials. Common examples of radiant heat include the way sunlight travels from the sun to warm the earth, the use of radiators in homes, and the warmth of incandescent light bulbs.

Skill 3.3 Calculate the amount of heat transfer by conduction or radiation, given appropriate data.

The amount of heat transferred by conduction through a material depends on several factors. It is directly proportional to the temperature difference ΔT between the surface from which the heat is flowing and the surface to which it is transferred. Heat flow H increases with the area A through which the flow occurs and also with the time duration t. The thickness of the material reduces the flow of heat. The relationship between all these variables is expressed as

$$H = \frac{k.t.A.\Delta T}{d}$$

where the proportionality constant k is known as the **thermal conductivity**, a property of the material. Thermal conductivity of a good conductor is close to 1 (0.97 cal/cm.s.^{0}C for silver) while good insulators have thermal conductivity that is nearly zero (0.0005 cal/cm.s.^{0}C for wood).

Problem: A glass window pane is 50 cm long and 30 cm wide. The glass is 1 cm thick. If the temperature indoors is $15^{0}C$ higher than it is outside, how much heat will be lost through the window in 30 minutes? The thermal conductivity of glass is 0.0025 cal/cm.s.^{0}C.

Solution: The window has area A = 1500 sq. cm and thickness d = 1 cm. Duration of heat flow is 1800 s and the temperature difference $\Delta T = 15^{0}C$. Therefore heat loss through the window is given by

$$H = (0.0025 \times 1800 \times 1500 \times 15)\,/\,1 = 101250 \text{ calories}$$

The amount of energy radiated by a body at temperature T and having a surface area A is given by the Stefan-Boltzmann law expressed as

$$I = e\sigma AT^4$$

where I is the radiated power in watts, e (a number between 0 and 1) is the **emissivity** of the body and σ is a universal constant known as **Stefan's constant** that has a value of $5.6703 \times 10^{-8} W/m^2.K^4$. Black objects absorb and radiate energy very well and have emissivity close to 1. Shiny objects that reflect energy are not good absorbers or radiators and have emissivity close to zero.

A body not only radiates thermal energy but also absorbs energy from its surroundings. The net power radiation from a body at temperature T in an environment at temperature T_0 is given by

$$I = e\sigma A(T^4 - T_0^4)$$

<u>Problem</u>: Calculate the net power radiated by a body of surface area 2 sq. m, temperature $30^\circ C$ and emissivity 0.5 placed in a room at a temperature of $15^\circ C$.

<u>Solution</u>: $I = 0.5 \times 5.67 \times 10^{-8} \times 2(303^4 - 288^4) = 88$ W

Skill 3.4 Interpret segments of graphs of temperature vs. heat added or removed (e.g., latent heats, specific heats).

The temperature of a material rises when heat is transferred to it and falls when heat is removed from it. When the material is undergoing a phase change (e.g. from solid to liquid), however, it absorbs or releases heat without a corresponding change in temperature. A **temperature vs. heat graph** can demonstrate these relationships visually. One can also calculate the specific heat or latent heat of phase change for the material by studying the details of the graph.

<u>Example</u>: The plot below shows heat applied to 1g of ice at -40C. The horizontal parts of the graph show the phase changes where the material absorbs heat but stays at the same temperature. The graph shows that ice melts into water at 0C and the water undergoes a further phase change into steam at 100C.

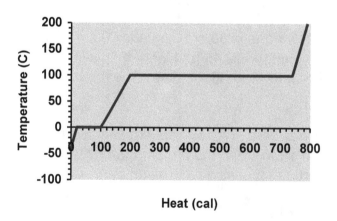

Heat (cal)

The specific heat of ice, water and steam and the latent heat of fusion and vaporization may be calculated from each of the five segments of the graph.

For instance, we see from the flat segment at temperature 0C that the ice absorbs 80 cal of heat. The latent heat L of a material is defined by the equation $\Delta Q = mL$ where ΔQ is the quantity of heat transferred and m is the mass of the material. Since the mass of the material in this example is 1g, the latent heat of fusion of ice is given by $L = \Delta Q / m = 80$ cal/g.

The next segment shows a rise in the temperature of water and may be used to calculate the specific heat C of water defined by $\Delta Q = mC\Delta T$, where ΔQ is the quantity of heat absorbed, m is the mass of the material and ΔT is the change in temperature. According to the graph, ΔQ = 200-100 =100 cal and ΔT = 100-0=100C. Thus, C = 100/100 = 1 cal/gC.

Problem: The plot below shows the change in temperature when heat is transferred to 0.5g of a material. Find the initial specific heat of the material and the latent heat of phase change.

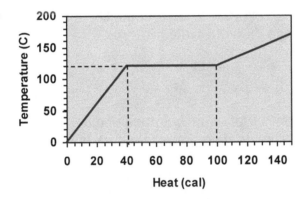

Solution: Looking at the first segment of the graph, we see that ΔQ = 40 cal and ΔT = 120 C. Since the mass m = 0.5g, the specific heat of the material is given by $C = \Delta Q / (m\Delta T)$ = 40/(0.5 X120) = 0.67 cal/gC.

The flat segment of the graph represents the phase change. Here ΔQ = 100 - 40=60 cal. Thus, the latent heat of phase change is given by $L = \Delta Q / m$ = 60/(0.5) = 120 cal/g.

Skill 3.5 Solve and analyze pressure, volume, and temperature relationships using the gas laws.

Boyle's law states that the volume of a fixed amount of gas at constant temperature is inversely proportional to the gas pressure, or:

$$V \propto \frac{1}{P}.$$

Gay-Lussac's law states that the pressure of a fixed amount of gas in a fixed volume is proportional to absolute temperature, or:

$$P \propto T.$$

Charles's law states that the volume of a fixed amount of gas at constant pressure is directly proportional to absolute temperature, or:

$$V \propto T.$$

The **combined gas law** uses the above laws to determine a proportionality expression that is used for a constant quantity of gas:

$$V \propto \frac{T}{P}.$$

The combined gas law is often expressed as an equality between identical amounts of an ideal gas at two different states ($n_1 = n_2$):

$$\frac{P_1 V_1}{T_1} = \frac{P_2 V_2}{T_2}.$$

Avogadro's hypothesis states that equal volumes of different gases at the same temperature and pressure contain equal numbers of molecules. **Avogadro's law** states that the volume of a gas at constant temperature and pressure is directly proportional to the quantity of gas, or:

$$V \propto n \text{ where } n \text{ is the number of moles of gas.}$$

Avogadro's law and the combined gas law yield $V \propto \frac{nT}{P}$. The proportionality constant R--the **ideal gas constant**--is used to express this proportionality as the **ideal gas law**:

1. $PV = nRT$.

The ideal gas law is useful because it contains all the information of Charles's, Avogadro's, Boyle's, and the combined gas laws in a single expression.

Solving ideal gas law problems is a straightforward process of algebraic manipulation. **Errors commonly arise from using improper units**, particularly for the ideal gas constant R. An absolute temperature scale must be used—never °C—and is usually reported using the Kelvin scale, but volume and pressure units often vary from problem to problem.

If pressure is given in atmospheres and volume is given in liters, a value for R of **0.08206 L- atm/(mol- K)** is used. If pressure is given in pascal (newtons/m²) and volume in m³, then the SI value for R of **8.314 J/(mol- K)** may be used because a joule is defined as a newton- meter or a pascal- m³. A value for R of **8.314 Pa- m³/(mol- K)** is identical to the ideal gas constant using joules.

The ideal gas law may also be rearranged to determine gas molar density in moles per unit volume (molarity):

$$\frac{n}{V} = \frac{P}{RT}.$$

Gas density d in grams per unit volume is found after multiplication by the molecular weight M:

$$d = \frac{nM}{V} = \frac{PM}{RT}.$$

Molecular weight may also be determined from the density of an ideal gas:

$$M = \frac{dV}{n} = \frac{dRT}{P}.$$

Example: Determine the molecular weight of an ideal gas that has a density of 3.24 g/L at 800 K and 3.00 atm.

Solution:
$$M = \frac{dRT}{P} = \frac{\left(3.24\ \frac{g}{L}\right)\left(0.08206\ \frac{L\text{-atm}}{mol\text{-}K}\right)(800\ K)}{3.00\ atm} = 70.9\ \frac{g}{mol}.$$

Tutorials for gas laws may be found online at: http://www.chemistrycoach.com/tutorials-6.htm. A flash animation tutorial for problems involving a piston may be found at http://www.mhhe.com/physsci/chemistry/essentialchemistry/flash/gasesv6.swf.

Skill 3.6 Calculate problems based upon the first law of thermodynamics (i.e., conservation of energy).

The first law of thermodynamics is a restatement of conservation of energy, i.e. the principle that energy cannot be created or destroyed. It also governs the behavior of a system and its surroundings. The change in heat energy supplied to a system (Q) is equal to the sum of the change in the internal energy (U) and the change in the work (W) done by the system against internal forces. Mathematically, we can express this as

$$\Delta Q = \Delta U + \Delta W$$

Let us examine a sample problem that relies upon this law.

A closed tank has a volume of 40.0 m³ and is filled with air at 25°C and 100 kPa. We desire to maintain the temperature in the tank constant at 25°C as water is pumped into it. How much heat will have to be removed from the air in the tank to fill the tank ½ full?

Solution: The problem involves isothermal compression of a gas, so $\Delta U_{gas}=0$. Consulting the equation above, $\Delta Q = \Delta U + \Delta W$, it is clear that the heat removed from the gas must be equal to the work done by the gas.

$$Q_{gas} = W_{gas} = P_{gas}V_1 \ln\left(\frac{V_2}{V_T}\right) = P_{gas}V_T \ln\left(\frac{\frac{1}{2}V_T}{V_T}\right) = P_{gas}V_T \ln \frac{1}{2}$$

$$= (100kPa)(40.0m^3)(-0.69314) = -2772.58kJ$$

Thus, the gas in the tank must lose 2772.58 kJ to maintain its temperature.

Skill 3.7 Calculate work from pressure vs. volume diagrams.

If the expansion or compression of a gas happens so slowly that the gas is always close to the equilibrium state, it is known as a **quasi-static process**. For an expansion or compression of this type, the state of the gas at each step of the process may be represented by its pressure and volume at that point. The work done by the gas or on the gas can be calculated from its *PV* diagram, i.e. the plot of the gas pressure vs. volume.

Consider a gas confined in a cylinder with a frictionless piston. In a quasi-static process, the piston moves very slowly without acceleration. If the area of the piston is *A* and it moves a distance *dx*, then the force exerted by the gas on the piston is *PA* and the work done by the gas is *PAdx*.

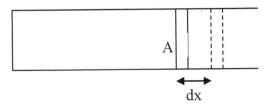

Since the change in volume of the gas *dV = Adx*, the work done by the gas is given by *dW = PAdx = PdV*. If the gas expands quasi-statically from volume *V1* to volume *V2*, the total work done is $W = \int_{V1}^{V2} PdV$. In a *PV* diagram, this expression represents the area under the pressure vs. volume curve.

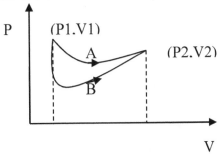

The work done by a gas is not determined only by its initial and final states but by the path through which the gas expands in the *PV* space. In the example diagram displayed above, a gas starts at pressure *P1* and volume *V1* and expands to volume *V2* at pressure *P2*. It is clear that if the gas expands through the path A, the area under the curve and the work done by the gas will be greater than the case where the gas expands through the path B.

Problem: If a gas expands from 1 liter to 2 liters at a constant pressure of 3 atmospheres, what is the work done by the gas?

Solution: Since pressure is constant, $W = P \int_{V11}^{V2} dV = P(V2 - V1) = 3(2-1) = 3$ L.atm.

Given that $1L = 10^{-3} m^3$ and 1 atm $= 101.3 \times 10^3 N/m^2$, $W = 303.9\,J.$

Skill 3.8 Identify and analyze processes in pressure vs. volume diagrams (e.g., isobaric process, isothermal process, adiabatic process).

For a gas in a state of equilibrium, the pressure P, volume V and temperature T are related through an equation of state. For a quasi-static process in which the gas remains close to equilibrium at all times, any two of these variables can characterize the state of the gas at a point in time. On a PV diagram, the state of a gas at any point is represented by its pressure P and volume V. Since P, V and T are related, when the volume changes through expansion or compression, either the pressure or temperature or both of these variables must change.

Processes where pressure remains constant are known as **isobaric** processes. These are represented by horizontal straight lines on a PV diagram.

Isothermal processes are those in which the temperature of the gas remains the same throughout. For an ideal gas $PV = nRT$ = constant. Thus the PV curve is a hyperbola. Since the temperature does not change, the internal energy of the gas remains constant and the heat Q absorbed by the gas is equal to the work W done by the gas.

During an **adiabatic** process no heat flows in or out of the gas. Thus the work done by the gas equals the decrease in internal energy of the gas and the temperature falls as the gas expands. The decrease in temperature leads to a greater decrease in pressure than in the case of isothermal expansion. As a result, the PV curve for adiabatic expansion of a gas is steeper than that for isothermal expansion.

Problem: The PV diagram below shows the quasi-static expansion of a gas from volume V1 to volume V2 through three different paths A, B and C, one adiabatic, one isothermal and one isobaric. Identify the process type of each path.

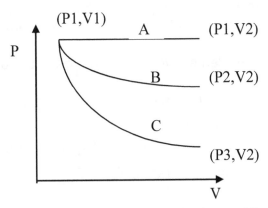

Solution: Path A is isobaric since it is a horizontal line with the pressure remaining constant at P1. Path C is adiabatic and path B is isothermal since adiabatic expansion leads to a steeper fall in pressure.

Skill 3.9 Determine the specific heat, latent heat, or temperatures of a substance, given appropriate calorimetric data.

The **internal energy** of a material is the **sum of the total kinetic energy** of its molecules and the **potential energy** of interactions between those molecules. Total kinetic energy includes the contributions from translational motion and other components of motion such as rotation. The potential energy includes **energy stored in the form of resisting intermolecular attractions** between molecules.

The **enthalpy** (*H*) of a material is the **sum of its internal energy and the mechanical work** it can do by driving a piston. A change in the **enthalpy** of a substance is the total **energy** change caused by **adding/removing heat** at constant pressure.

When a material is heated and experiences a phase change, **thermal energy is used to break the intermolecular bonds** holding the material together. Similarly, bonds are formed with the release of thermal energy when a material changes its phase during cooling. Therefore, **the energy of a material increases during a phase change that requires heat and decreases during a phase change that releases heat**. For example, the energy of H_2O increases when ice melts and decreases when water freezes.

<u>Heat capacity and specific heat</u>
A substance's molar **heat capacity** is the heat required to **change the temperature of one mole of the substance by one degree**. Heat capacity has units of joules per mol- kelvin or joules per mol- °C. The two units are interchangeable because we are only concerned with differences between one temperature and another. A Kelvin degree and a Celsius degree are the same size.

The **specific heat** of a substance (also called specific heat capacity) is the heat required to **change the temperature of one gram or kilogram by one degree.** Specific heat has units of joules per gram-°C or joules per kilogram-°C.

These terms are used to solve problems involving a change in temperature by applying the formula:
$q = n \times C \times \Delta T$ where $q \Rightarrow$ heat added (positive) or evolved (negative)

$\qquad n \Rightarrow$ amount of material

$\qquad C \Rightarrow$ molar heat capacity if *n* is in moles, specific heat if *n* is a mass

$\qquad \Delta T \Rightarrow$ change in temperature $T_{final} - T_{initial}$

Example:

What is the change in energy of 10 g of gold at 25 °C when it is heated beyond its melting point to 1300 °C. You will need the following data for gold:

Solid heat capacity: 28 J/mol-K

Molten heat capacity: 20 J/mol-K

Enthalpy of fusion: 12.6 kJ/mol

Melting point: 1064 °C

Solution: First determine the number of moles used: $10 \text{ g} \times \dfrac{1 \text{ mol}}{197 \text{ g}} = 0.051 \text{ mol}$.

There are then three steps. 1) Heat the solid. 2) Melt the solid. 3) Heat the liquid. All three require energy so they will be positive numbers.

1) Heat the solid:

$$q_1 = n \times C \times \Delta T = 0.051 \text{ mol} \times 28 \ \frac{J}{\text{mol-K}} \times (1064 \ ^\circ C - 25 \ ^\circ C)$$

$$= 1.48 \times 10^3 \text{ J} = 1.48 \text{ kJ}$$

2) Melt the solid: $q_2 = n \times \Delta H_{fusion} = 0.051 \text{ mol} \times 12.6 \ \frac{kJ}{mol}$

$$= 0.64 \text{ kJ}$$

3) Heat the liquid:

$$q_3 = n \times C \times \Delta T = 0.051 \text{ mol} \times 20 \frac{J}{\text{mol-K}} \times (1300 \ ^\circ C - 1064 \ ^\circ C)$$

$$= 2.4 \times 10^2 \text{ J} = 0.24 \text{ kJ}$$

The sum of the three processes is the total change in energy of the gold:

$$q = q_1 + q_2 + q_3 = 1.48 \text{ kJ} + 0.64 \text{ kJ} + 0.24 \text{ kJ} = 2.36 \text{ kJ}$$

$$= 2.4 \text{ kJ}$$

Skill 3.10 Apply the second law of thermodynamics (entropy) to physical situations.

To understand the second law of thermodynamics, we must first understand the concept of entropy. Entropy is the transformation of energy to a more disordered state and is the measure of how much energy or heat is available for work. The simplest statement of the second law of thermodynamics is that the entropy of an isolated system not in equilibrium tends to increase over time. The entropy approaches a maximum value at equilibrium. This, then, has two major implications:

1. No machine is 100% efficient.
2. Heat cannot spontaneously pass from a colder to a hotter object.

Below are several common examples in which we see the manifestation of the second law.

- The diffusion of molecules of perfume out of an open bottle
- Even the most carefully designed engine releases some heat and cannot convert all the chemical energy in the fuel into mechanical energy
- A block sliding on a rough surface slows down
- An ice cube sitting on a hot sidewalk melts into a little puddle; we must provide energy to a freezer to facilitate the creation of ice

When discussing the second law, scientists often refer to the "arrow of time". This is to help us conceptualize how the second law forces events to proceed in a certain direction. To understand the direction of the arrow of time, consider some of the examples above; we would never think of them as proceeding in reverse. That is, as time progresses, we would never see a puddle in the hot sun spontaneously freeze into an ice cube or the molecules of perfume dispersed in a room spontaneously re-concentrate themselves in the bottle. Similarly a "psychological arrow of time" is the reason we can remember the past but not the future.

Skill 3.11 Relate temperature to kinetic molecular theory.

The relationship between **kinetic energy** and **intermolecular forces** determines whether a collection of molecules will be a gas, liquid, or solid. In a gas, the energy of intermolecular forces is much weaker than the kinetic energy of the molecules. Kinetic molecular theory is usually applied to gases and is best applied by imagining ourselves shrinking down to become a molecule and picturing what happens when we bump into other molecules and into container walls.

Gas **pressure** results from molecular collisions with container walls. The **number of molecules** striking an **area** on the walls and the **average kinetic energy** per molecule are the only factors that contribute to pressure. A higher **temperature** increases speed and kinetic energy. There are more collisions at higher temperatures, but the average distance between molecules does not change, and thus density does not change in a sealed container.

Kinetic molecular theory explains why the pressure and temperature of gases behave the way they do by making a few assumptions, namely:

1) The energies of intermolecular attractive and repulsive forces may be neglected.
2) The average kinetic energy of the molecules is proportional to absolute temperature.
3) Energy can be transferred between molecules during collisions and the collisions are elastic, so the average kinetic energy of the molecules doesn't change due to collisions.
4) The volume of all molecules in a gas is negligible compared to the total volume of the container.

Strictly speaking, molecules also contain some kinetic energy by rotating or experiencing other motions. The motion of a molecule from one place to another is called **translation**. Translational kinetic energy is the form that is transferred by collisions, and kinetic molecular theory ignores other forms of kinetic energy because they are not proportional to temperature.

The following table summarizes the application of kinetic molecular theory to an increase in container volume, number of molecules, and temperature:

Effect of an **increase** in one variable with other two constant	Impact on gas: − = decrease, **0** = no change, **+** = increase						
	Average distance between molecules	Density in a sealed container	Average speed of molecules	Average translational kinetic energy of molecules	Collisions with container walls per second	Collisions per unit area of wall per second	Pressure (P)
Volume of container (V)	+	−	0	0	−	−	−
Number of molecules	−	+	0	0	+	+	+
Temperature (T)	0	0	+	+	+	+	+

Additional details on the kinetic molecular theory may be found at http://hyperphysics.phy-astr.gsu.edu/hbase/kinetic/ktcon.html. An animation of gas particles colliding is located at http://comp.uark.edu/~jgeabana/mol_dyn/.

COMPETENCY IV. KNOWLEDGE OF MECHANICS

Skill 4.1   Interpret the one-dimensional motion of an object, given distance/time, velocity/time, or acceleration/time graphs.

The relationship between time, position or distance, velocity and acceleration can be understood conceptually by looking at a graphical representation of each as a function of time. Simply, the velocity is the slope of the position vs. time graph and the acceleration is the slope of the velocity vs. time graph. If you are familiar with calculus then you know that this relationship can be generalized: velocity is the first derivative and acceleration the second derivative of position.

Here are three examples:

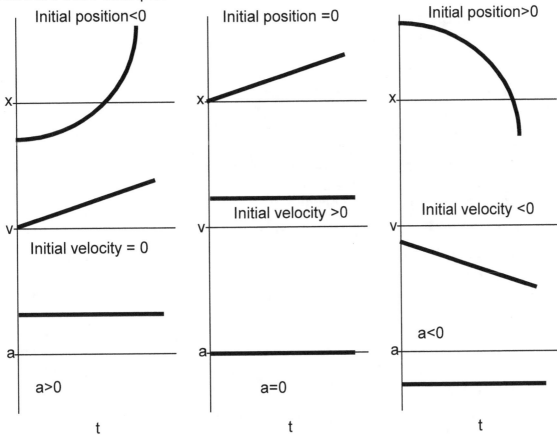

There are three things to notice:
1) In each case acceleration is constant. This isn't always the case, but a simplification for this illustration.
2) A non-zero acceleration produces a position curve that is a parabola.
3) In each case the initial velocity and position are specified separately. The acceleration curve gives the shape of the velocity curve, but not the initial value and the velocity curve gives the shape of the position curve but not the initial position.

Skill 4.2 Calculate distance, velocity, acceleration, or time of objects moving in one dimension.

Kinematics is the part of mechanics that seeks to understand the motion of objects, particularly the relationship between position, velocity, acceleration and time.

$X < 0$ $X = 0$ $X > 0$

The above figure represents an object and its displacement along one linear dimension.

First we will define the relevant terms:

1. Position or Distance is usually represented by the variable x. It is measured relative to some fixed point or datum called the origin in linear units, meters, for example.

2. Displacement is defined as the change in position or distance which an object has moved and is represented by the variables D, d or Δx. Displacement is a vector with a magnitude and a direction.

3. Velocity is a vector quantity usually denoted with a V or v and defined as the rate of change of position. Typically units are distance/time, m/s for example. Since velocity is a vector, if an object changes the direction in which it is moving it changes its velocity even if the speed (the scalar quantity that is the magnitude of the velocity vector) remains unchanged.

i) Average velocity: $\vec{V} \equiv \frac{\Delta d}{\Delta t} = d_1 - d_0 / t_1 - t_0.$

The ratio, $\Delta d / \Delta t$ is called the average velocity. Average here denotes that this quantity is defined over a period Δt.

ii) Instantaneous velocity is the velocity of an object at a particular moment in time. Conceptually, this can be imagined as the extreme case when Δt ☐ is infinitely small.

4. Acceleration represented by a is defined as the rate of change of velocity and the units are m/s^2. Both an average and an instantaneous acceleration can be defined similarly to velocity.

From these definitions we develop the kinematic equations. In the following, subscript i denotes initial and subscript f denotes final values for a time period. Acceleration is assumed to be constant with time.

$$v_f = v_i + at \qquad (1)$$

$$d = v_i t + \frac{1}{2} at^2 \qquad (2)$$

$$v_f^2 = v_i^2 + 2ad \qquad (3)$$

$$d = \left(\frac{v_i + v_f}{2} \right) t \qquad (4)$$

Example:
Leaving a traffic light a man accelerates at 10 m/s². a) How fast is he going when he has gone 100 m? b) How fast is he going in 4 seconds? C) How far does he travel in 20 seconds.

Solution:
a) Use equation 3. He starts from a stop so $v_i=0$ and $v_f^2=2 \times 10m/s^2 \times 100m=2000 \ m^2/s^2$ and $v_f=45$ m/s.
b) Use equation 1. Initial velocity is again zero so $v_f=10m/s^2 \times 4s=40$ m/s.
c) Use equation 2. Initial velocity is again zero so $d=1/2 \times 10 \ m/s^2 \times (20s)^2= 2000$ m

Skill 4.3   Calculate distance, velocity, acceleration, or time of objects moving in two dimensions (e.g., projectile motion).

In skill IV – 2, we discussed the relationships between distance, velocity, acceleration and time and the four simple equations that relate these quantities when acceleration is constant (e.g. in cases such as gravity). In two dimensions the same relationships apply, but each dimension must be treated separately. Now we will discuss motion in two dimensions. Let us take a look at scalar and vector quantities.

The most common example of an object moving in two dimensions is a projectile. A projectile is an object upon which the only force acting is gravity. Some examples:
i) An object dropped from rest.
ii) An object thrown vertically upwards at an angle
iii) A canon ball.

Once a projectile has been put in motion (say, by a canon or hand) the only force acting it is gravity, which near the surface of the earth implies it experiences $a=g=9.8m/s^2$.

This is most easily considered with an example such as the case of a bullet shot horizontally from a standard height at the same moment that a bullet is dropped from exactly the same height. Which will hit the ground first? If we assume wind resistance is negligible, then the acceleration due to gravity is our only acceleration on either bullet and we must conclude that they will hit the ground at the same time. The horizontal motion of the bullet is not affected by the downward acceleration.

Example:
I shoot a projectile at 1000 m/s from a perfectly horizontal barrel exactly 1 m above the ground. How far does it travel before hitting the ground?

<u>Solution:</u>

First figure out how long it takes to hit the ground by analyzing the motion in the vertical direction. In the vertical direction, the initial velocity is zero so we can rearrange kinematic equation 2 from the previous section to give:

$$t = \sqrt{\frac{2d}{a}}$$. Since our displacement is 1 m and a=g=9.8m/s^2, t=0.45 s.

Now use the time to hitting the ground from the previous calculation to calculate how far it will travel horizontally. Here the velocity is 1000m/s and there is no acceleration. So we simple multiply velocity with time to get the distance of 450m.

Skill 4.4   Relate linear kinematic equations to situations involving circular motion (e.g., tangential speed, tangential acceleration, centripetal acceleration).

In a previous section we defined the kinematic variables and studied the kinematic equations applied to objects moving with a constant acceleration. Of course, not all moving objects move in a linear fashion, many often undergo rotational motion. Motion on an arc can also be considered from the view point of the kinematic equations.

As pointed out earlier, displacement, velocity and acceleration are all vector quantities, i.e. they have magnitude (the speed is the magnitude of the velocity vector) and direction. This means that if one drives in a circle at constant speed one still experiences an acceleration that changes the direction. We can define a couple of parameters for objects moving on circular paths and see how they relate to the kinematic equations.

1. Tangential speed: The tangent to a circle or arc is a line that intersects the arc at exactly one point. If you were driving in a circle and instantaneously moved the steering wheel back to straight, the line you would follow would be the tangent to the circle at the point where you moved the wheel. The tangential speed then is the instantaneous magnitude of the velocity vector as one moves around the circle.

2. Tangential acceleration: The tangential acceleration is the component of acceleration that would change the tangential speed and this can be treated as a linear acceleration if one imagines that the circular path is unrolled and made linear.

3. Centripetal acceleration: Centripetal acceleration corresponds to the constant change in the direction of the velocity vector necessary to maintain a circular path. Always acting toward the center of the circle, centripetal acceleration has a magnitude proportional to the tangential speed squared divided by the radius of the path.

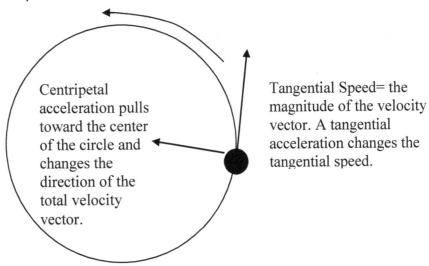

Centripetal acceleration pulls toward the center of the circle and changes the direction of the total velocity vector.

Tangential Speed= the magnitude of the velocity vector. A tangential acceleration changes the tangential speed.

Skill 4.5   Apply Newton's first or second laws to solve problems.

Newton's first law of motion: "An object at rest tends to stay at rest and an object in motion tends to stay in motion with the same speed and in the same direction unless acted upon by an unbalanced force". Prior to Newton's formulation of this law, being at rest was considered the natural state of all objects, because at the earth's surface we have the force of gravity working at all times which causes nearly any object put into motion to eventually come to rest. Newton's brilliant leap was to recognize that an unbalanced force changes the motion of a body, whether that body begins at rest or at some non-zero speed.

We experience the consequences of this law everyday. For instance, the first law is why seat belts are necessary to prevent injuries. When a car stops suddenly, say by hitting a road barrier, the driver continues on forward until acted upon by a force. The seat belt provides that force and distributes the load across the whole body rather than allowing the driver to fly forward and experience the force against the steering wheel.

Newton's second law of motion: "The acceleration of an object as produced by a net force is directly proportional to the magnitude of the net force, in the same direction as the net force, and inversely proportional to the mass of the object". In the equation form, it is stated as $F = ma$, force equals mass times acceleration. It is important to remember that this is the net force and that forces are vector quantities. Thus if an object is acted upon by 12 forces that sum to zero, there is no acceleration. Also, this law embodies the idea of inertia as a consequence of mass. For a given force, the resulting acceleration is proportionally smaller for a more massive object because the larger object has more inertia.

The first two laws are generally applied together via the equation **F=ma.** The first law is largely the conceptual foundation for the more specific and quantitative second law.

Example: For the arrangement shown, find the force necessary to overcome the 500 N force pushing to the left and move the truck to the right with an acceleration of 5 m/s².

500 N 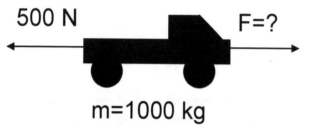 F=?

m=1000 kg

Solution: Since we know the acceleration and mass, we can calculate the net force necessary to move the truck with this acceleration. Assuming that to the right is the positive direction we sum the forces and get
F-500N = 1000kg x 5 m/s². Solving for F, we get 5500 N.

Skill 4.6 Apply Newton's third law to physical situations

Newton's third law: **"For every action, there is an equal and opposite reaction".**
This statement means that in every interaction, there is a pair of forces acting on the two interacting objects. The size of the force on the first object equals the size of the force on the second object. The direction of the force on the first object is opposite to the direction of the force on the second object.

1. The propulsion/movement of fish through water: A fish uses its fins to push water backwards. The water pushes back on the fish. Because the force on the fish is unbalanced the fish moves forward.
2. The motion of car: A car's wheels push against the road and the road pushes back. Since the force of the road on the car is unbalanced the car moves forward.
3. Walking: When one pushes backwards on the foot with the muscles of the leg, the floor pushes back on the foot. If the forces of the leg on the foot and the floor on the foot are balanced, the foot will not move and the muscles of the body can move the other leg forward.

Skill 4.7 Solve and analyze conservation of momentum problems in one or two dimensions.

The law of conservation of momentum states that the total momentum of an *isolated system* (not affected by external forces and not having internal dissipative forces) always remains the same. For instance, in any collision between two objects in an isolated system, the total momentum of the two objects after the collision will be the same as the total momentum of the two objects before the collision. In other words, any momentum lost by one of the objects is gained by the other. In one dimension this is easy to visualize.

Imagine two carts rolling towards each other as in the diagram below

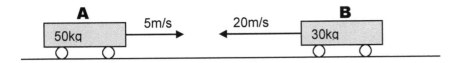

Before the collision, cart **A** has 250 kg m/s of momentum, and cart **B** has –600 kg m/s of momentum. In other words, the system has a total momentum of –350 kg m/s of momentum.

After the collision, the two cards stick to each other, and continue moving. How do we determine how fast, and in what direction, they go?

We know that the new mass of the cart is 80kg, and that the total momentum of the system is −350 kg m/s. Therefore, the velocity of the two carts stuck together must be $\frac{-350}{80} = -4.375\,m/s$

Conservation of momentum works the same way in two dimensions, the only change is that you need to use vector math to determine the total momentum and any changes, instead of simple addition.

Imagine a pool table like the one below. Both balls are 0.5 kg in mass.

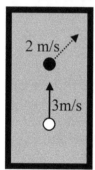

Before the collision, the white ball is moving with the velocity indicated by the solid line and the black ball is at rest.

After the collision the black ball is moving with the velocity indicated by the dashed line (a 135° angle from the direction of the white ball).

With what speed, and in what direction, is the white ball moving after the collision?

$p_{white/before} = .5 \cdot (0,3) = (0,1.5)$ $p_{black/before} = 0$ $p_{total/before} = (0,1.5)$

$p_{black/after} = .5 \cdot (2\cos 45, 2\sin 45) = (0.71, 0.71)$

$p_{white/after} = (-0.71, 0.79)$

i.e. the white ball has a velocity of $v = \sqrt{(-.71)^2 + (0.79)^2} = 1.06\,m/s$

and is moving at an angle of $\theta = \tan^{-1}\left(\frac{0.79}{-0.71}\right) = -48°$ from the horizontal

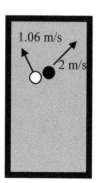

Skill 4.8   Solve problems using the impulse-momentum theorem.

The impulse-momentum theorem states that any impulse acting on a system changes the momentum of that system. When considering the impulse-momentum theorem, there are several factors that need to be taken into account. The first factor is that momentum is a vector quantity $p = m \cdot v$. It has both magnitude and direction. Therefore, any action that causes either the speed or the direction of an object to change causes a change in its momentum. An impulse is defined as a force acting over a period of time, and any impulse acting on the system will change its momentum, as you can see from the equations below:

$$F = m \cdot a \rightarrow F = m \cdot \frac{\Delta v}{t} \rightarrow F \cdot t = m \cdot \Delta v$$

i.e. Forces acting over time cause a change in momentum.

<u>Sample Problems</u>:

1. A 1 kg ball is rolled towards a wall at 4 m/s. It hits the wall, and bounces back off the wall at 3 m/s.

a. What is the change in velocity?

   The velocity goes from +4m/s to –3m/s, a net change of -7m/s.

b. At what point does the impulse occur?

   The impulse occurs when the ball hits the wall.

2. A 30kg woman is in a car accident. She was driving at 50m/s when she had to hit the brakes to avoid hitting the car in front of her.

    a. The automatic tensioning device in her seatbelt slows her down to a stop over a period of one half second. How much force does it apply?

$$F = m \cdot \frac{\Delta v}{t} \rightarrow F = 30 \cdot \frac{50}{.5} = 3000N$$

    b. If she hadn't been wearing a seatbelt, the windshield would have stopped her in .001 seconds. How much force would have been applied there?

$$F = m \cdot \frac{\Delta v}{t} \rightarrow F = 30 \cdot \frac{50}{.001} = 1500000N$$

Skill 4.9 Solve and analyze problems using Newton's universal law of gravitation.

Newton's universal law of gravitation states that any two objects experience a force between them as the result of their masses. Specifically, the force between two masses m_1 and m_2 can be summarized as

$$F = G\frac{m_1 m_2}{r^2}$$

where G is the gravitational constant ($G = 6.672 \times 10^{-11} Nm^2 / kg^2$), and r is the distance between the two objects.

The weight of an object is the result of the gravitational force of the earth acting on its mass. The acceleration due to Earth's gravity on an object is 9.81 m/s². Since force equals mass * acceleration, the magnitude of the gravitational force created by the earth on an object is

$$F_{Gravity} = m_{object} \cdot 9.81 \frac{m}{s^2}$$

Important things to remember:

1. The gravitational force is proportional to the masses of the two objects, but *inversely* proportional to the *square of the distance* between the two objects.
2. When calculating the effects of the acceleration due to gravity for an object above the earth's surface, the distance above the surface is ignored because it is inconsequential compared to the radius of the earth. The constant figure of 9.81 m/s² is used instead.

Problem: Two identical 4 kg balls are floating in space, 2 meters apart. What is the magnitude of the gravitational force they exert on each other?

Solution:

$$F = G\frac{m_1 m_2}{r^2} = G\frac{4 \times 4}{2^2} = 4G = 2.67 \times 10^{-10} \, N$$

Skill 4.10 Solve and analyze problems involving the effect of friction on the motion of an object.

In the real world, whenever an object moves its motion is opposed by a force known as friction. How strong the frictional force is depends on numerous factors such as the roughness of the surfaces (for two objects sliding against each other) or the viscosity of the liquid an object is moving through. Most problems involving the effect of friction on motion deal with sliding friction. This is the type of friction that makes it harder to push a box across cement than across a marble floor.

When you try and push an object from rest, you must overcome the maximum **static friction** force to get it to move. Once the object is in motion, you are working against **kinetic friction** which is smaller than the static friction force previously mentioned. Sliding friction is primarily dependent on two things, the **coefficient of friction (μ)** which is primarily dependent on roughness of the surfaces involved and the amount of force pushing the two surfaces together. This force is also known as the **normal force (Fn)**, the perpendicular force between two surfaces. When an object is resting on a flat surface, the normal force is pushing opposite to the gravitational force – straight up. When the object is resting on an incline, the normal force is less (because it is only opposing that portion of the gravitational force acting perpendicularly to the object) and its direction is perpendicular to the surface of incline but at an angle from the ground. Therefore, for an object experiencing no external action, the magnitude of the normal force is either equal to or less than the magnitude of the gravitational force **(Fg)** acting on it. The frictional force **(Ff)** acts perpendicularly to the normal force, opposing the direction of the object's motion.

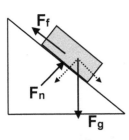

The frictional force is normally directly proportional to the normal force and, unless you are told otherwise, can be calculated as **Ff = μ Fn** where μ is either the coefficient of static friction or kinetic friction depending on whether the object starts at rest or in motion. In the first case, the problem is often stated as "how much force does it take to start an object moving" and the frictional force is given by **Ff > μs Fn** where μs is the coefficient of static friction. When questions are of the form "what is the magnitude of the frictional force opposing the motion of this object," the frictional force is given by **Ff = μk Fn** where μk is the coefficient of kinetic friction.

There are several important things to remember when solving problems about friction.

1. The frictional force acts in opposition to the direction of motion.
2. The frictional force is proportional, and acts perpendicular to, the normal force.
3. The normal force is perpendicular to the surface the object is lying on. If there is a force pushing the object against the surface, it will increase the normal force.

Problem:

A woman is pushing an 800N box across the floor. She pushes with a force of 1000 N. The coefficient of kinetic friction is 0.50. If the box is already moving, what is the force of friction acting on the box?

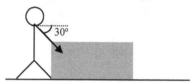

Solution:

First it is necessary to solve for the normal force.

F_n= 800N + 1000N (sin 30°) = 1300N
Then, since $F_f = \mu \, F_n$ = 0.5*1300=650N

Skill 4.11 Solve and analyze problems involving work, energy, and power.

In physics, work is defined as force times distance $W = F \cdot s$. Work is a scalar quantity, it does not have direction, and it is usually measured in Joules ($N \cdot m$). It is important to remember, when doing calculations about work, that the only part of the force that contributes to the work is the part that acts in the direction of the displacement. Therefore, sometimes the equation is written as $W = F \cdot s \cos \theta$, where θ is the angle between the force and the displacement.

Problem:
A man uses 6N of force to pull a 10kg block, as shown below, over a distance of 3 m. How much work did he do?

Solution:

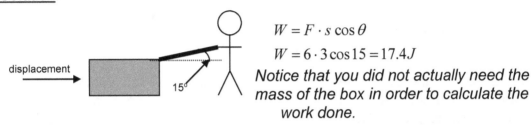

$$W = F \cdot s \cos \theta$$
$$W = 6 \cdot 3 \cos 15 = 17.4 J$$
Notice that you did not actually need the mass of the box in order to calculate the work done.

Power is defined in relationship to work. It is the rate at which work is done, or, in other words, the amount of work done in a certain period of time: $P = W/t$. There are many different measurements for power, but the one most commonly seen in physics problems is the Watt which is measured in Joules per second. Another commonly discussed unit of power is horsepower, and 1hp=746 W.

Problem:

A woman standing in her 4th story apartment raises a 10kg box of groceries from the ground using a rope. She is pulling at a constant rate, and it takes her 5 seconds to raise the box one meter. How much power is she using to raise the box?

Solution:

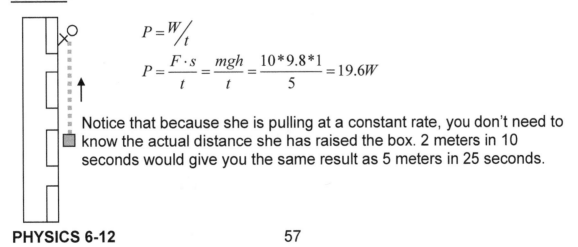

$$P = W/t$$
$$P = \frac{F \cdot s}{t} = \frac{mgh}{t} = \frac{10 * 9.8 * 1}{5} = 19.6W$$

Notice that because she is pulling at a constant rate, you don't need to know the actual distance she has raised the box. 2 meters in 10 seconds would give you the same result as 5 meters in 25 seconds.

Energy is also defined, in relation to work, as the ability of an object to do work. As such, it is measured in the same units as work, usually Joules. Most problems relating work to energy are looking at two specific kinds of energy. The first, kinetic energy, is the energy of motion. The heavier an object is and the faster it is going, the more energy it has resulting in a greater capacity for work. The equation for kinetic energy is : $KE = \frac{1}{2}mv^2$.

Problem:

A 1500 kg car is moving at 60m/s down a highway when it crashes into a 3000kg truck. In the moment before impact, how much kinetic energy does the car have?

Solution:

$$KE = \frac{1}{2}mv^2 = \frac{1}{2} \cdot 1500 \cdot 60^2 = 2.7 \times 10^6 J$$

The other form of energy frequently discussed in relationship to work is gravitational potential energy, or potential energy, the energy of position. Potential energy is calculated as $PE = mgh$ where h is the distance the object is capable of falling.

Problem:

Which has more potential energy, a 2 kg box held 5 m above the ground or a 10 kg box held 1 m above the ground?

Solution:

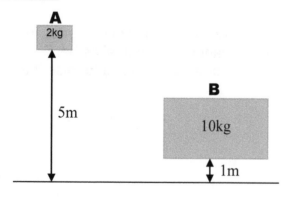

$$PE_A = mgh = 2 \cdot g \cdot 5 = 10g$$
$$PE_B = mgh = 10 \cdot g \cdot 1 = 10g$$
$$PE_A = PE_B$$

Skill 4.12 Solve and analyze problems involving two connected masses.

When solving problems involving two connected masses, it is necessary to understand the geometry of their connection. Specifically, it is important to know the location of the center of mass of the combined object because that is where the mass of an object is considered to act for the purpose of calculating torque. The center of mass for a system containing two rigidly connected masses is located along the line connecting the two objects' individual centers of mass. Its distance from the first mass can be calculated as $r_1 = d \cdot \dfrac{m_2}{m_1 + m_2}$.

Example:

If the spheres below are 2m apart, how far is the center of mass of the system from the 5 kg sphere?

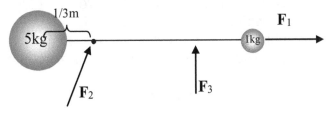

$$r_1 = d \cdot \frac{m_2}{m_1 + m_2} = 2 \cdot \frac{1}{6} = \frac{1}{3} m$$

Knowing the location of the center of mass of two connected objects also allows you to calculate the behavior of the system when forces are applied at different locations on the system. For example, any unbalanced force applied through the center of mass ($\mathbf{F}_1$ and $\mathbf{F}_2$ below) will induce linear motion but not rotational motion. In contrast, unbalanced forces that don't go through the center of mass ($\mathbf{F}_3$ below) will induce a torque around the center of mass, as well as (potentially) linear motion.

<u>Problem</u>:

Two kids, Sam and Anna, are sitting on a seesaw. Sam weighs 16kg and Anna weighs 8kg. They each sit exactly 1m from the pivot point. What is the net torque on the seesaw and where does it act?

<u>Solution:</u>

The net torque is simple to calculate in this case,

$$\tau = mgL_{sam} - mgL_{anna} = 16 \cdot 9.8 \cdot 1 - 8 \cdot 9.8 \cdot 1$$
$$= 78.4 N \cdot m$$

However, the net torque **acts** from the center of mass – which is at

$$r_1 = d \cdot \frac{m_2}{m_1 + m_2} = 2 \cdot \frac{8}{24} = \frac{2}{3} m \text{ from Sam, or } \frac{1}{3} \text{m from the pivot point.}$$

Skill 4.13 Solve and analyze equilibrium problems involving torque.

Torque is rotational motion about an axis. It is defined as $\tau = L \times F$, where L is the lever arm. The length of the lever arm is calculated by measuring the perpendicular line drawn from the line of force to the axis of rotation.

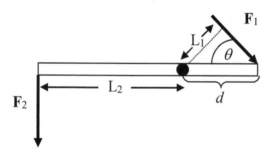

By convention, torques that act in a clockwise direction are considered negative and those in a counterclockwise direction are considered positive. In order for an object to be in equilibrium, the sum of the torques acting on it must be zero.

The equation that would put the above figure in equilibrium is $F_1 L_1 = -F_2 L_2$ (please note that in this case $L_1 = d \sin \theta$).

Examples:
Some children are playing with the spinner below, when one young boy decides to pull on the spinner arrow in the direction indicated by F_1. How much torque does he apply to the spinner arrow?

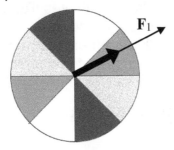

$\tau = L \times F$, but L=0 because the line of force goes directly through the axis of rotation (i.e. the perpendicular distance from the line of force to the pivot point is 0). Therefore the boy applies no torque to the spinner.

In the system diagrammed below, find out what the magnitude of F_1 must be in order to keep the system in equilibrium.

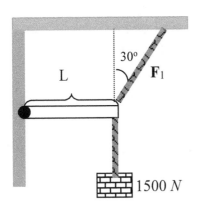

$$F_1 L = -F_2 L$$

$$F_{1x} L + F_{1y} L = -(-1500L) \dots \text{but } F_{1x} = 0 *$$

$$F_{1y} L = 1500L$$

$$F_1 \cos 30 L = 1500L$$

$$(0.866) F_1 = 1500$$

$$F_1 = 1732N$$

the effect of $F_{1x}=0$ because that portion of the force goes right through the pivot and causes no torque.

Things to remember:
1. When writing the equation for a body at equilibrium, the point chosen for the axis of rotation is arbitrary.
2. The center of gravity is the point in an object where its weight can be considered to act for the purpose of calculating torque.
3. The lever arm, or moment arm, of a force is calculated as the **perpendicular** distance from the line of force to the pivot point/axis of rotation.
4. Counterclockwise torques are considered positive while clockwise torques are considered negative.

Skill 4.14   Solve and analyze problems involving rotational systems in terms of angular momentum and conservation of rotational energy.

Linear motion is measured in rectangular coordinates. Rotational motion is measured differently, in terms of the angle of displacement. There are three common ways to measure rotational displacement; degrees, revolutions, and radians. Degrees and revolutions have an easy to understand relationship, one revolution is 360°. Radians are slightly less well known and are defined as $\dfrac{arc\ length}{radius}$. Therefore 360°=2π radians and 1 radian = 57.3°.

The major concepts of linear motion are duplicated in rotational motion with linear displacement replaced by the angle of displacement.

Angular velocity ω = angular displacement / time

Also, the linear velocity v of a rolling object can be written as $v = r\omega$.

One important difference in the equations relates to the use of mass in rotational systems. In rotational problems, not only is the mass of an object important but also its location. In order to include the spatial distribution of the mass of the object, a term called **moment of inertia** is used, $I = m_1 r_1^{\,2} + m_2 r_2^{\,2} + \cdots + m_n r_n^{\,2}$

Example:

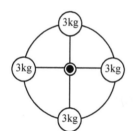

If the radius of the wheel on the left is 0.75m, what is its moment of inertia?

$$I = 3 \cdot 0.75^2 + 3 \cdot 0.75^2 + 3 \cdot 0.75^2 + 3 \cdot 0.75^2 = 6.75$$

Note: $I_{Sphere} = \dfrac{2}{5} mr^2,\ I_{Hoop/\,Ring} = mr^2,\ I_{disk} = \dfrac{1}{2} mr^2$

A related concept is the radius of gyration (k), which is the average distance of mass from the center of an object. $k_{Sphere} = \sqrt{\dfrac{2}{5}} r,\ k_{Hoop/\,Ring} = r,\ k_{disk} = \dfrac{r}{\sqrt{2}}$. As you can see $I = mk^2$

Angular momentum (L), and rotational kinetic energy (KE_r), are therefore defined as follows: $L = I\omega,\quad KE_r = \dfrac{1}{2} I\omega^2$

As with all systems, energy is conserved unless the system is acted on by an external force. This can be used to solve problems such as the one below:

Example:

A uniform ball of radius r and mass m starts from rest and rolls down a frictionless incline of height h. When the ball reaches the ground, how fast is it going?

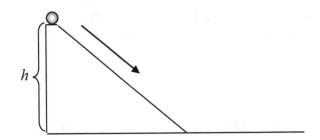

$$PE_{initial} + KE_{rotational\,initial} + KE_{linear/\,initial} = PE_{final} + KE_{rotational\,final} + KE_{linear/\,final}$$

$$mgh + 0 + 0 = 0 + \frac{1}{2}I\omega_{final}^2 + \frac{1}{2}mv_{final}^2 \rightarrow mgh = \frac{1}{2} \cdot \frac{2}{5}mr^2\omega_{final}^2 + \frac{1}{2}mv_{final}^2$$

$$mgh = \frac{1}{5}mr^2(\frac{v_{final}}{r})^2 + \frac{1}{2}mv_{final}^2 \rightarrow mgh = \frac{1}{5}mv_{final}^2 + \frac{1}{2}mv_{final}^2$$

$$gh = \frac{7}{10}v_{final}^2 \rightarrow v_{final} = \sqrt{\frac{10}{7}gh}$$

Similarly, unless a net torque acts on a system, the angular momentum remains constant in both magnitude and direction. This can be used to solve many different types of problems including ones involving satellite motion.

Example:
A planet of mass m is circling a star in an orbit like the one below. If its velocity at point A is 60,000m/s, and r_B=8 r_A, what is its velocity at point B?

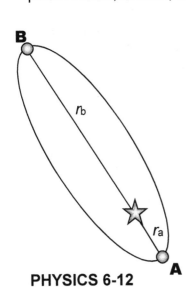

$$I_B\omega_B = I_A\omega_A$$

$$mr_B^2\omega_B = mr_A^2\omega_A$$

$$r_B^2\omega_B = r_A^2\omega_A$$

$$r_B^2\frac{v_B}{r_B} = r_A^2\frac{v_A}{r_A}$$

$$r_B v_B = r_A v_A$$

$$8r_A v_B = r_A v_A$$

$$v_B = \frac{v_A}{8} = 7500m/s$$

Skill 4.15 Solve and analyze problems involving the work-energy theorem.

The work-energy theorem states that the amount of work done on an object is equal to its change in mechanical energy (kinetic or potential energy). Specifically, in systems where multiple forces are at work, the energy change of the system is the work done by the *net* force on the object. Problems dealing with the work-energy theorem may look at changes in kinetic energy, changes in potential energy, or some combination of the two. It is also important to remember that only external forces can cause changes in an object's total amount of mechanical energy. Internal forces, such as spring force or gravity, only lead to conversions between kinetic and potential energy rather than changes in the total level of mechanical energy.

Example:

1. A woman driving a 2000 kg car along a level road at 30 m/s takes her foot off the gas to see how far her car will roll before it slows to a stop. She discovers that it takes 150m. What is the average force of friction acting on the car?

$$W = \Delta KE$$

$$f \cdot s \cos \theta = \tfrac{1}{2} mv_{final}^2 - \tfrac{1}{2} mv_{initial}^2$$

$$f \cdot 150 \cdot (-1) = \tfrac{1}{2} \cdot 2000 \cdot 0^2 - \tfrac{1}{2} \cdot 2000 \cdot 30^2$$

$$-150f = -900000$$

$$f = 6000N$$

According to the work-energy theorem, the amount of work done on the car is equal to the change in its mechanical energy which in this case is its change in kinetic energy. Since the only force acting on the car is friction, all the work can be attributed to the frictional force. It is important to realize, for this problem, that the force of friction is against the direction of motion, and thus cosθ = -1.

2. A 20kg child lifts his .5 kg ball off the floor to put it away on his bookshelf 1.5 meters above the ground. How much work has he done?

$$W = \Delta PE$$

$$W = mgh_{final} - mgh_{initial}$$

$$W = mg(h_{final} - h_{initial}) = .5 \cdot 9.8 \cdot 1.5 = 7.35J$$

Skill 4.16 Analyze problems involving the relationship between depth, density of fluid, and pressure.

The weight of a column of fluid creates hydrostatic pressure. Common situations in which we might analyze hydrostatic pressure include tanks of fluid, a swimming pool, or the ocean. Also, atmospheric pressure is an example of hydrostatic pressure.

Because hydrostatic pressure results from the force of gravity interacting with the mass of the fluid or gas, it is governed by the following equation:

$$P = \rho g h$$

where P=hydrostatic pressure
ρ=density of the fluid
g=acceleration of gravity
h=height of the fluid column

Example: How much pressure is exerted by the water at the bottom of a 5 meter swimming pool filled with water?

Solution: We simply use the equation from above, recalling that the acceleration due to gravity is 9.8m/s² and the density of water is 1000 kg/m³.

$$P = \rho g h = 1000 \frac{kg}{m^3} \times 9.8 \frac{m}{s^2} \times 5m = 49{,}000 Pa = 49 kPa$$

Skill 4.17 Solve and analyze problems concerning the buoyant force on a submerged or floating object (e.g., Archimedes' principle).

Archimedes discovered through observation that, for an object in a fluid, "the upthrust is equal to the weight of the displaced fluid" and the weight of displaced fluid is directly proportional to the volume of displaced fluid. The second part of his discovery is useful when we want to, for instance, determine the volume of an oddly shaped object. We determine its volume by immersing it in a graduated cylinder and measuring how much fluid is displaced. We explore his first observation in more depth below.

Today, we call Archimedes' "upthrust" **buoyancy**. Buoyancy is the force produced by a fluid on a fully or partially immersed object. The buoyant force (F_buoyant) is found using the following equation:

$$F_{bouyant} = \rho V g$$

where ρ=density of the fluid

V=volume of fluid displaced by the submerged object
g=the acceleration of gravity

Notice that the buoyant force opposes the force of gravity. For an immersed object, a gravitational force (equal to the object's mass times the acceleration of gravity) pulls it downward, while a buoyant force (equal to the weight of the displaced fluid) pushes it upward.

Also note that, from this principle, we can predict *whether* an object will sink or float in a given liquid. We can simply compare the density of the material from which the object is made to that of the liquid. If the material has a lower density, it will float; if it has a higher density it will sink. Finally, if an object has a density equal to that of the liquid, it will neither sink nor float.

Example: Will gold (ρ=19.3 g/cm³) float in water?

Solution: We must compare the density of gold with that of water, which is 1 g/cm³.

$$\rho_{gold} > \rho_{water}$$

So, gold will sink in water.

Example: Imagine a 1 m³ cube of oak (530 kg/m³) floating in water. What is the buoyant force on the cube and how far up the sides of the cube will the water be?

Solution: Since the cube is floating, it has displaced enough water so that the buoyant force is equal to the force of gravity. Thus the buoyant force on the cube is equal to its weight 1X530X9.8 N = 5194 N.

To determine where the cube sits in the water, we simply the find the ratio of the wood's density to that of the water:

$$\frac{\rho_{oak}}{\rho_{water}} = \frac{530\,^{kg}/_{m^3}}{1000\,^{kg}/_{m^3}} = 0.53$$

Thus, 53% of the cube will be submerged. Since the edges of the cube must be 1m each, the top 0.47m of the cube will appear above the water.

Skill 4.18 Solve and analyze problems involving moving fluid (e.g., mass conservation, Bernoulli's principle).

The study of moving fluid is contained within fluid mechanics which is itself a component of continuum mechanics. Some of the most important applications of fluid mechanics involve liquids and gases moving in tubes and pipes. To understand the movement of fluids, one of the first quantities we must define is volumetric flow rate which may have units of gallons per min (gpm), liters/s, cubic feet per min (cfm), gpf, or m³/s:

$$Q = Av\cos\theta$$

Where Q=volumetric flow rate
A=cross sectional area of the pipe
v=fluid velocity
θ=the angle between the direction of the fluid flow and a vector normal to A

Note that in situations in which the fluid velocity is perpendicular to the cross sectional area, this equation is simply:

$$Q = Av$$

It is also convenient to sometimes discuss mass flow rate ($\dot{m}$), which we can easily find using the density (ρ) of the fluid:

$$\dot{m} = \rho v A = \rho Q$$

Usually, we make an assumption that the fluid is incompressible, that is, the density is constant. Like many commonly used simplifications, this assumption is largely and typically correct though real fluids are, of course, compressible to varying extents. When we do assume that density is constant, we can use conservation of mass to determine that when a pipe is expanded or restricted, the mass flow rate will remain the same. Let's see how this pertains to an example:

Given conservation of mass, it must be true that:

$$v_1 A_1 = v_2 A_2$$

Note that this means the fluid will flow faster in the narrower portions of the pipe and more slowly in the wider regions. An everyday example of this principle is seen when one holds their thumb over the nozzle of a garden hose; the cross sectional area is reduced and so the water flows more quickly.

Much of what we know about fluid flow today was originally discovered by Daniel Bernoulli. His most famous discovery is known as Bernoulli's Principle which states that, if no work is performed on a fluid or gas, an increase in velocity will be accompanied by a decrease in pressure. The mathematical statement of the Bernoulli's Principle for incompressible flow is:

$$\frac{v^2}{2} + gh + \frac{p}{\rho} = \text{constant}$$

where v= fluid velocity
g=acceleration due to gravity
h=height
p=pressure
ρ=fluid density

Though some physicists argue that it leads to the compromising of certain assumptions (i.e., incompressibility, no flow motivation, and a closed fluid loop), most agree it is correct to explain "lift" using Bernoulli's principle. This is because Bernoulli's principle can also be thought of as predicting that the pressure in moving fluid is less than the pressure in fluid at rest. Thus, there are many examples of physical phenomenon that can be explained by Bernoulli's Principle:

- The lift on airplane wings occurs because the top surface is curved while the bottom surface is straight. Air must therefore move at a higher velocity on the top of the wing and the resulting lower pressure on top accounts for lift.
- The tendency of windows to explode rather than implode in hurricanes is caused by the pressure drop that results from the high speed winds blowing across the outer surface of the window. The higher pressure on the inside of the window then pushes the glass outward, causing an explosion.
- The ballooning and fluttering of a tarp on the top of a semi-truck moving down the highway is caused by the flow of air across the top of the truck. The decrease in pressure causes the tarp to "puff up."
- A perfume atomizer pushes a stream of air across a pool of liquid. The drop in pressure caused by the moving air lifts a bit of the perfume and allows it to be dispensed.

Skill 4.19 Solve and analyze problems involving center of mass.

The center of mass is the position in space about which the mass of a system is evenly distributed. It is calculated by summing the product of each object's mass with its position and dividing by the total mass of the system. Knowing how to calculate the center of mass is important because forces which act at a distance (such as gravity) act through an object or system's center of mass. The center of mass can be thought of as the point where an equivalent mass of infinitely small size would be located.

Example in one dimension:

Center of mass = (5kg x -2m + 1kg x 6m)/6kg = -0.66m

Example in two dimensions:

In this example we have 4 masses numbered 1-4.

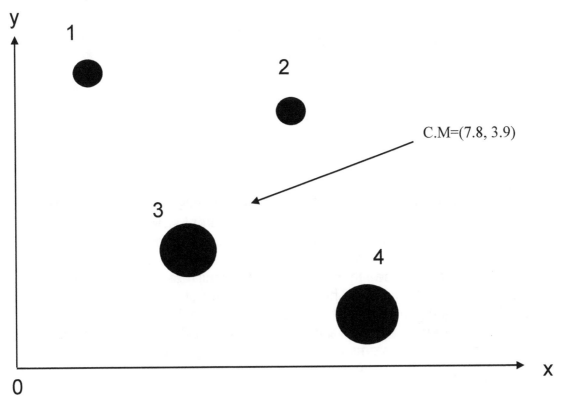

Particle	X position	Y position	Mass
1	1 m	10 m	1 kg
2	9 m	9 m	1.5 kg
3	5 m	4 m	4 kg
4	11 m	1 m	5 kg

We repeat the analysis for the one dimensional case in each dimension.
C.M. in x =
(1m x 1 kg + 9m x 1.5kg + 5m x 4kg + 11m x 5 kg)/(1 kg + 1.5 kg + 4 kg + 5 kg)=
7.8m
C.M. in y=
(10m x 1 kg + 9m x 1.5kg + 4m x 4kg + 1m x 5 kg)/(1 kg + 1.5 kg + 4 kg + 5 kg)=
3.9m

In the case of three dimensions we would extend the above strategy repeating the one-dimensional calculation in each direction.

Problem: Determine the gravitational attraction between System 1 and System 2 in this one dimensional example.

System 1   System 2

Solution: Rather than calculating the gravitational force of each object in system 1 on each object in System 2, we will apply the principle of action of center of mass to solve this problem. Each object has a different size, but its position on the line is the position of its center of mass. Therefore, its contribution to the mass of the system can be considered to be located at the center of mass. Looking at System 1 we see that the two equal small masses are located equidistant from the large one. Therefore, the center of mass of System 1 is the center of mass of the large object at x =0. System 1 is thus equivalent to a system of one object at x=0 with a mass of 11,000 kg. The gravitational attractive force between the two systems is, F_g= (G x 11,000 kg x 5000 kg)/(25 m)^2
=88,000 x 6.672×10^{-11} N = $5.9 \times 10^{-6} N$.

Skill 4.20 Analyze the forces acting on an object, using a free-body diagram.

Free body diagrams are simple sketches that show all the objects and forces in a given physical situation. This makes them very useful for understanding and solving physical problems. These diagrams show relative positions, masses, and the direction in which forces are acting.

Below are two examples of free body diagrams. While we did not previously define them as free body diagrams, we have already used them in the preceding sections (e.g. 5-10, 5-12) to help us solve sample problems.

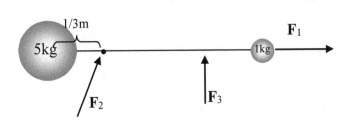
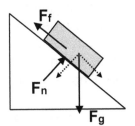

COMPETENCY V.   KNOWLEDGE OF VIBRATION, WAVES, AND SOUND

Skill 5.1   Identify and apply wave terminology (e.g., velocity, frequency, amplitude, wavelength, period, pitch, intensity, phase, nodes, antinodes, transverse waveforms, and longitudinal waveforms).

To fully understand waves, it is important to understand many of the terms used to characterize them.

Wave velocity: Two velocities are used to describe waves. The first is phase velocity, which is the rate at which a wave propagates. For instance, if you followed a single crest of a wave, it would appear to move at the phase velocity. The second type of velocity is known as group velocity and is the speed at which variations in the wave's amplitude shape propagate through space. Group velocity is often conceptualized as the velocity at which energy is transmitted by a wave. Phase velocity is denoted v_p and group velocity is denoted v_g.

Crest: The maximum value that a wave assumes; the highest point.

Trough: The lowest value that a wave assumes; the lowest point.

Nodes: The points on a wave with minimal amplitude.

Antinodes: The farthest point from the node on the amplitude axis; both the crests and the troughs are antinodes.

Amplitude: The distance from the wave's highest point (the crest) to the equilibrium point. This is a measure of the maximum disturbance caused by the wave and is typically denoted by A.

Wavelength: The distance between any two sequential troughs or crests denoted λ and representing a complete cycle in the repeated wave pattern.

Period: The time required for a complete wavelength or cycle to pass a given point. The period of a wave is usually denoted T.

Frequency: The number of periods or cycles per unit time (usually a second). The frequency is denoted f and is the inverse of the wave's period (that is, $f=1/T$).

Phase: This is a given position in the cycle of the wave. It is most commonly used in discussing a "being out of phase" or a "phase shift", an offset between waves.

Transverse waves: Waves in which the oscillations are perpendicular to the direction in which in the wave travels.

Longitudinal waves: Waves in which the oscillations are in the direction in which the wave travels.

Polarization: A property of transverse waves that describes the plane perpendicular to the direction of travel in which the oscillation occurs. Note that longitudinal waves are not polarized because they can oscillate only in one direction, the direction of travel.

Pitch: The frequency of a sound wave as perceived by the human ear. A high pitch sound corresponds to a high frequency sound wave and a low pitch sound corresponds to a low frequency sound wave.

Sound power: This is the sonic energy of a sound wave per unit time.

Sound intensity: This is simply the sound power per unit area.

We can visualize several of these terms on the following diagram of a simple, periodic sine wave on a scale of distance displacement (x-axis) vs. (y-axis):

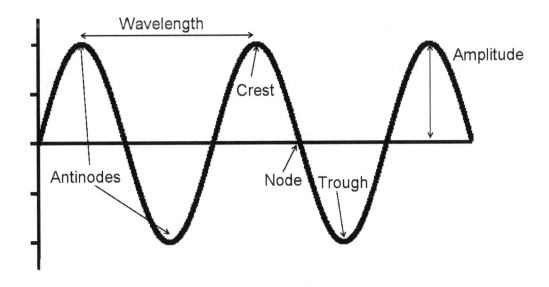

Skill 5.2 Analyze the motion of particles in a medium in the presence of transverse and longitudinal waves.

The distance that a particle in a medium moves as a wave is transmitted through it is measured by particle displacement. Particle displacement can be measured in both transverse and longitudinal waves.

In a longitudinal wave, particle displacement is parallel to the wave's direction of travel. Thus, if we imagine a longitudinal waveform moving down a tube, particles will move back and forth parallel to the sides of the tube. Sound is one of the most important types of longitudinal waves and the described phenomenon is manifest as sound travels through air or water.

Transverse waves, on the other hand, oscillate in a direction perpendicular to the direction of wave travel. So let's imagine the same tube, this time with a transverse wave traveling down it. In this case, the particles oscillate up and down within the tube. Particle displacement in a transverse wave can also be easily visualized in the vibration of a taut string.

Excellent videos that demonstrate the movement of individual particles are available at the following web address:
http://www.kettering.edu/~drussell/Demos/waves/wavemotion.html

Finally, it is important to note that, in either type of wave, particle displacement depends on the particle velocity of the wave in the medium which is not the same as the velocity of the wave itself.

Skill 5.3   Identify factors that affect mechanical wave propagation and wave speed.

Mechanical waves differ from electromagnetic waves in that they need a medium through which to travel. This medium can be a solid, as in the case of the waves in a Slinky toy, a gas, such as a sound wave traveling to your ear, or liquid, such waves in the ocean. It follows, then, that mechanical waves cannot exist in a vacuum.

Mechanical waves rely on the local oscillation of each atom in a medium, but the material itself does not move; only the energy is transferred from atom to atom. Therefore the material through which the mechanical wave is traveling greatly affects the wave's propagation and speed. In particular, a material's elastic constant and density affect the speed at which a wave travels through it. Both of these properties of a medium can predict the extent to which the atoms will vibrate and pass along the energy of the wave. The general relationship between these properties and the speed of a wave in a solid is given by the following equation:

$$V = \sqrt{\frac{C_{ij}}{\rho}}$$

where V is the speed of sound, C_{ij} is the elastic constant, and ρ is the material density. It is worth noting that the elastic constant differs depending on direction in anisotropic materials and the ij subscripts indicate that this directionality must be taken into account.

A mechanical wave requires an initial energy input to be created. Once this initial energy is added, the wave will travel through the medium until all the energy has been dissipated. This initial amount of energy upon creation of the wave will also affect the extent of its propagation throughout the medium.

The type of mechanical wave is another factor that will determine propagation. There are three types of mechanical waves. Transverse waves are waves that cause the medium to vibrate at a 90 degree angle to the direction of travel of the wave. The next type is a longitudinal wave which causes the medium to vibrate in the same direction as the direction of travel of the wave. When the particles of the medium the longitudinal wave is traveling through are drawn close together it is called compression. When the particles of the medium it is traveling through are spread apart, it is called rarefaction. The final type of wave is a surface wave. This type of wave travels along a surface that is between two mediums. An example of a surface wave would be waves in a pool, or in an ocean.

Skill 5.4 Identify and analyze characteristics and examples of simple harmonic motion (e.g., oscillating springs, vibrating strings, pendulum).

Harmonic motion or harmonic oscillation is seen in any system that follows Hooke's Law. Hooke's law simply predicts the behavior of certain bodies as they return to equilibrium following a displacement. It is given by the following equation:

$$F = -kx$$

Where F=restoring force
     x=displacement
     k=a positive constant

From this equation we can see that the harmonic motion is neither damped nor driven. Harmonic motion is observed as sinusoidal oscillations about an equilibrium point. Both the amplitude and the frequency are constant. Further, the amplitude is always positive and is a function of the original force that disrupted the equilibrium. If an object's oscillation is governed solely by Hooke's law, it is a simple harmonic oscillator. Below are examples of simple harmonic oscillators:

Pendula: A pendulum is a mass on the end of a rigid rod or a string. An initial push will cause the pendulum to swing back and forth. This motion will be harmonic as long as the pendulum moves through an angle of less than 15°.

Masses connected to springs: A spring is simply the familiar helical coil of metal that is used to store mechanical energy. In a typical system, one end of a spring is attached to a mass and the other to a solid surface (a wall, ceiling, etc).

If the spring is then stretched or compressed (i.e., removed from equilibrium) it will oscillate harmonically.

Vibrating strings: A string or rope tied tightly at both ends will oscillate harmonically when it is struck or plucked. This is often the mechanism used to generate sound in string-based instruments such as guitars and pianos.

Several simple harmonic oscillations maybe superimposed to create complex harmonic motion. The best-known example of complex harmonic motion is a musical chord.

View an animation of harmonic oscillation here:

http://en.wikipedia.org/wiki/Image:Simple_harmonic_motion_animation.gif

Skill 5.5 Analyze interference as the superposition of waves and apply to beats, standing waves, and interference patterns.

Interference occurs when two or more waves are superimposed. Usually, interference is observed in coherent waves, well-correlated waves that have very similar frequencies or even come from the same source.

Superposition of waves may result in either constructive or destructive interference. Constructive interference occurs when the crests of the two waves meet at the same point in time. Conversely, destructive interference occurs when the crest of one wave and the trough of the other meet at the same point in time. It follows, then, that constructive interference increases amplitude and destructive interference decreased it. We can also consider interference in terms of wave phase; waves that are out of phase with one another will interfere destructively while waves that are in phase with one another will interfere constructively. In the case of two simple sine waves with identical amplitudes, for instance, amplitude will double if the waves are exactly in phase and drop to zero if the waves are exactly 180° out of phase.

Additionally, interference can create a standing wave, a wave in which certain points always have amplitude of zero. Thus, the wave remains in a constant position. Standing waves typically results when two waves of the same frequency traveling in opposite directions through a single medium are superposed. View an animation of how interference can create a standing wave at the following

URL:http://www.glenbrook.k12.il.us/GBSSCI/PHYS/mmedia/waves/swf.html

All wavelengths in the EM spectrum can experience interference but it is easy to comprehend instances of interference in the spectrum of visible light. One classic example of this is Thomas Young's double-slit experiment. In this experiment a beam of light is shone through a paper with two slits and a striated wave pattern results on the screen. The light and dark bands correspond to the areas in which the light from the two slits has constructively (bright band) and destructively (dark band) interfered.

Similarly, we may be familiar with examples of interference in sound waves. When two sounds waves with slightly different frequencies interfere with each other, beat results. We hear a beat as a periodic variation in volume with a rate that depends on the difference between the two frequencies. You may have observed this phenomenon when listening to two instruments being tuned to match; beating will be heard as the two instruments approach the same note and disappear when they are perfectly in tune.

Skill 5.6   Solve and analyze problems involving standing waves (e.g., open or closed tube, vibrating string).

A standing wave typically results from the interference between two waves of the same frequency traveling in opposite directions. The result is a stationary vibration pattern. One of the key characteristics of standing waves is that there are points in the medium where no movement occurs. The points are called nodes and the points where motion is maximal are called antinodes. This property allows for the analysis of various typical standing waves.

Vibrating string
Imagine a string of length L tied tightly at its two ends. We can generate a standing wave by plucking the string. The waves traveling along the string are reflected at the fixed end points and interfere with each other to produce standing waves. There will always be two nodes at the ends where the string is tied. Depending on the frequency of the wave that is generated, there may also be other nodes along the length of the string. In the diagrams below, examples are given of strings with 0, 1, or 2 additional nodes. These vibrations are known as the 1st, 2nd, and 3rd harmonics. The higher order harmonics follow the same pattern although they are not diagramed here.

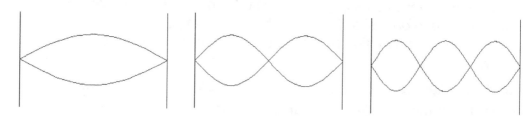

Since we know the length of the string (L) in each case, we can calculate the wavelength (λ) and frequency (f) for any harmonic using the following formula, where n=the harmonic order (n=1,2,3...) and v is the phase velocity of the wave.

$$\lambda_n = \frac{2L}{n} \qquad\qquad f_n = \frac{v}{\lambda_n} = n\frac{v}{2L}$$

Waves in a tube
Just as on a string, standing waves can propagate in gaseous or liquid medium inside a tube. In these cases we will also observe harmonic vibrations, but their nature will depend on whether the ends of the tube are closed or open.

Specifically, an antinode will be observed at an open end and a node will appear at a closed end. Then, just as in the string example above, we can derive formulas that allow us to predict the wavelength and frequency of the harmonic vibrations that occur in a tube. Below, only frequencies are given; wavelength can be found by applying the formula f=v/λ.

For a tube with two closed ends or two open ends (note that this is the same as for the string described above):

$$f_n = \frac{nv}{2L}$$

where n = 1,2,3,4...

When only one end of a tube is closed, that end become a node and wave exhibits odd harmonics. For a tube with one close end and one open end:

$$f_n = \frac{nv}{4L}$$

where n = 1,3,5,7...

An animation at the following URL may be helpful in visualizing these various standing waves:
http://www.physics.smu.edu/~olness/www/05fall1320/applet/pipe-waves.html

Skill 5.7   Interpret the decibel scale as it relates to sound intensity.

The decibel scale is used to measure sound intensity. It originated in a unit known as the bel which is defined as the reduction in audio level over 1 mile of a telephone cable. Since the bel describes such a large variation in sound, it became more common to use the decibel, which is equal to 0.1 bel. A decibel value is related to the intensity of a sound by the following equation:

$$X_{dB} = 10 \log_{10}\left(\frac{X}{X_0}\right)$$

Where X_{dB} is the value of the sound in decibels
   X is the intensity of the sound
   X_0 is a reference value with the same units as X. X_0 is commonly taken to be the threshold of hearing at $10^{-12} W/m^2$.

It is important to note the logarithmic nature of the decibel scale and what this means for the relative intensity of sounds. The perception of the intensity of sound increases logarithmically, not linearly. Thus, an increase of 10 dB corresponds to an increase by one order of magnitude. For example, a sound that is 20 dB is not twice as loud as sound that is 10 dB; rather, it is 10 times as loud. A sound that is 30 dB will the 100 times as loud as the 10 dB sound.

Finally, let's equate the decibel scale with some familiar noises. Below are the decibel values of some common sounds.
Whispering voice: 20 dB
Quiet office: 60 dB
Traffic: 70 dB
Cheering football stadium: 110 dB
Jet engine (100 feet away): 150 dB
Space shuttle liftoff (100 feet away): 190 dB

Skill 5.8 Apply the Doppler effect to physical situations (e.g., change in wave characteristics due to relative motion of source, media, or receiver).

The Doppler effect is the name given to the perceived change in frequency that occurs when the observer or source of a wave is moving. Specifically, the perceived frequency increases when a wave source and observer move toward each other and decreases when a source and observer move away from each other. Thus, the source and/or observer velocity must be factored in to the calculation of the perceived frequency. The mathematical statement of this effect is:

$$f' = f_0 \left(\frac{v \pm v_o}{v \pm v_s} \right)$$

where f'= observed frequency
f_0= emitted frequency
v= the speed of the waves in the medium
v_s= the velocity of the source (positive in the direction away from the observer)
v_o= the velocity of the observer (positive in the direction towards the source)

Note that any motion that changes the perceived frequency of a wave will cause the Doppler effect to occur. Thus, the wave source, the observer position, or the medium through which the wave travels could possess a velocity that would alter the observed frequency of a wave. You may view animations of stationary and moving wave sources at the following URL:

http://www.kettering.edu/~drussell/Demos/doppler/doppler.html

So, let's consider two examples involving sirens and analyze what happens when either the source or the observer moves. First, imagine a person standing on the side of a road and a police car driving by with its siren blaring. As the car approaches, the velocity of the car will mean sound waves will "hit" the observer as the car comes closer and so the pitch of the sound will be high. As it passes, the pitch will slide down and continue to lower as the car moves away from the observer. This is because the sound waves will "spread out" as the source recedes. Now consider a stationary siren on the top of fire station and a person driving by that station. The same Doppler effect will be observed: the person would hear a high frequency sound as he approached the siren and this frequency would lower as he passed and continued to drive away from the fire station.

The Doppler effect is observed with all types of electromagnetic radiation. In everyday life, we may be most familiar with the Doppler effect and sound, as in the example above. However, we can observe example of it throughout the EM spectrum. For instance, the Doppler effect for light has been exploited by astronomers to measure the speed at which stars and galaxies are approaching. Another familiar application is the use of Doppler radar by police to detect the speed of on coming cars.

Skill 5.9   Analyze waves as functions of positions and time using both graphical and mathematical representations, and relate to physical examples.

Waves are simply disturbances that propagate through space and time. Most waves must propagate through a medium, which may be solid, liquid, or gas. However, some electromagnetic waves do not require a medium and can move through a vacuum. Most waves transfer energy from their source to their destination, typically without actually transferring molecules of the medium through which they travel. All around us, there are examples of waves including ocean waves, sound, radio waves, microwaves, seismic waves, sunlight, x-rays, and radioactive gamma rays. Whether these waves actually displace media or simply carry energy, their positions fluctuate as they move through time and space. Often these fluctuations are regular and we can use both diagrams and mathematical equations to understand the pattern a wave follows in space and how quickly it moves.

This diagram and the terms within were introduced in section V-1 above. This diagram of a sinusoidal wave shows us displacement caused by the wave as it propagates through a medium. This displacement can be graphed against either time or distance. Note how displacement depends on the distance which the wave has traveled/ how much time has elapsed. So if we chose a particular displacement (let's say the crest), the wave will return to that displacement value (i.e., crest again) after one period (T) or one wavelength (λ).

The general equation for a wave is a partial differential equation which can be simplified to express the behavior of commonly encountered harmonic waveforms. For instance, for a standing wave:

$$y(z,t) = A(z,t)\sin(kz - \omega t + \phi)$$

where y=displacement
z=distance
t=time
k=wave number
ω=angular frequency
ϕ=phase
A(z,t)=the amplitude envelope of the wave

The important concept to note is that y is a function of both z and t. This means that the wave's position depends on both time and distance, just as was seen in the diagram above.

Skill 5.10 Analyze reflection and refraction of waves in physical situations.

Wave refraction is a change in direction of a wave due to a change in its speed. This most commonly occurs when a wave passes from one material to another, such as a light ray passing from air into water or glass. However, light is only one example of refraction; any type of wave can undergo refraction. Another example would be physical waves passing from water into oil.

At the boundary of the two media, the wave velocity is altered, the direction changes, and the wavelength increases or decreases. However, the frequency remains constant.

The refractive indices (related to the wave velocity) of the two media through which the wave passes determine the extent of the refraction. Snell's law describes the relationship between the refractive indices of the media and the angles in each medium between the ray and the normal to the surface between the media:

$$n_1 \sin\theta_1 = n_2 \sin\theta_2$$

where n_i represents the index of refraction in medium i, and θ_i represents the angle the light makes with the normal in medium i.

Reflection is the change in direction of a wave at an interface between two dissimilar media such that the wave returns into the medium from which it originated. The most common example of this is light waves reflecting from a mirror, but sound and water waves can also be reflected. The law of reflection states that the angle of incidence is equal to the angle of reflection.

Reflection may occur whenever a wave travels from a medium of a given refractive index to another medium with a different index. A certain fraction of the light is reflected from the interface and the remainder is refracted. However, when the wave is moving from a dense medium into one less dense, that is the refractive index of the first is greater than the second, a critical angle exists which will create a phenomenon known as total internal reflection. In this situation all of the wave is reflected. When a wave reflects off a more dense material (higher refractive index) than that from which it originated, it undergoes a 180° phase change. In contrast, a less dense, lower refractive index material will reflect light in phase.

COMPETENCY VI.   KNOWLEDGE OF LIGHT AND OPTICS

Skill 6.1   Identify the evidence that the properties of light can be explained by particle and/or wave characteristics.

Scientists have argued for years whether light is a wave or a stream of particles. Actually, light exhibits the behaviors of both waves and particles.

Wave characteristics
Light undergoes **reflection**, **refraction**, and **diffraction** just as any wave would. The image you see in a mirrored surface is the result of the reflection of the light waves off the surface. Light waves follow the "law of reflection," i.e. the angle at which the light wave approaches a flat reflecting surface is equal to the angle at which it leaves the surface. When light crosses the boundary between two different media, its path is bent, or refracted. Diffraction occurs when light encounters an obstacle in its path or passes through an opening. Light diffracts around the sides of an object causing the shadow of the object to appear fuzzy (**interference effects**).

Another phenomenon unique to waves is **wave interference**. This characteristic describes what happens when two waves meet while traveling along the same medium. If light **constructively interferes** (trough meets trough or crest meets crest), the two light waves reinforce one another to produce a stronger light wave. However, if light **destructively interferes** (crest meets trough), the two light waves destroy each other and no light wave is produced.

Polarization changes unpolarized light into polarized light. This process can only occur with a transverse wave. An everyday example of polarization is found in polarized sunglasses which reduce glare.

Particle characteristics
Einstein came up with the quantum theory of light that states that light is made up of **photons** or **quanta**, discrete particles of electromagnetic radiation. The photons, or individual particles of light, have been shown to have isolated arrival times. A movie was taken of the comet Hyakutake that showed a breakdown of the photons traveling with the comet and scattered throughout the region. Some phenomena such as **blackbody radiation** and the **photoelectric effect** can only be explained using the particle nature of light.

Presently, a combination of the two theories, or **wave - particle duality,** is accepted.

Skill 6.2 Solve and analyze refraction problems (e.g., index of refraction, Snell's law).

Index of refraction

Light travels at different speeds in different media. The speed of light in a vacuum is represented by

$$c = 2.99792458 \times 10^8 \, m/s$$

but is usually rounded to

$$c = 3.00 \times 10^8 \, m/s.$$

Light will never travel faster than this value. The **index of refraction**, n, is the amount by which light slows in a given material and is defined by the formula

$$n = \frac{c}{v}$$

where v represents the speed of light through the given material.

Problem: The speed of light in an unknown medium is measured to be $1.24 \times 10^8 \, m/s$. What is the index of refraction of the medium?

Solution:

$$n = \frac{c}{v}$$

$$n = \frac{3.00 \times 10^8}{1.24 \times 10^8} = 2.42$$

Referring to a standard table showing indices of refraction, we would see that this index corresponds to the index of refraction for diamond.

Snell's Law

Snell's Law describes how light bends, or refracts, when traveling from one medium to the next. It is expressed as

$$n_1 \sin \theta_1 = n_2 \sin \theta_2$$

where n_i represents the index of refraction in medium i, and θ_i represents the angle the light makes with the normal in medium i.

Problem: The index of refraction for light traveling from air into an optical fiber is 1.44. (a) In which direction does the light bend? (b) What is the angle of refraction inside the fiber, if the angle of incidence on the end of the fiber is 22°?

Solution: (a) The light will bend toward the normal since it is traveling from a rarer region (lower n) to a denser region (higher n).

(b) Let air be medium 1 and the optical fiber be medium 2:

$$n_1 \sin\theta_1 = n_2 \sin\theta_2$$
$$(1.00)\sin 22° = (1.44)\sin\theta_2$$
$$\sin\theta_2 = \frac{1.00}{1.44}\sin 22° = (.6944)(.3746) = 0.260$$
$$\theta_2 = \sin^{-1}(0.260) = 15°$$

The angle of refraction inside the fiber is $15°$.

Skill 6.3   Interpret the relationships between wavelength, frequency, and velocity of light.

The speed of light c is equal to the distance traveled divided by time taken. Since the light wave travels the distance of one wavelength λ in the period of the wave T,

$$c = \frac{\lambda}{T}$$

The frequency of a wave, f, is the number of completed periods in one second. In general,

$$f = \frac{1}{T}$$

So the formula for the speed of light can be rewritten as

$$c = \lambda f$$

The speed of the wave is equal to the wavelength times the frequency.

Skill 6.4   Analyze the effects of linear polarizing filters on the polarization and intensity of light.

Linear polarizing filters have the effect they do because of their chemical makeup. They are composed of long-chain molecules aligned in the same direction. As unpolarized light strikes the filter, the portion of the light waves, or electromagnetic vibrations, that are aligned parallel to the direction of the molecules are absorbed.

The alignment of these molecules creates a polarization axis that extends across the length of the filter. Only those vibrations that are parallel to the axis are allowed to pass through; other vibrations are blocked.

Example: A polarizing filter with a horizontal axis will allow the portion of the light waves that are aligned horizontally to pass through the filter and will block the portion of the light waves that are aligned vertically. One-half of the light is being blocked or conversely, one-half of the light is being absorbed. The image being viewed is not distorted but dimmed.

Example: If two filters are used, one with a horizontal axis and one with a vertical axis, all light will be blocked.

Skill 6.5   Solve problems and analyze situations involving images produced by plane or curved mirrors.

Plane mirrors

Problem: If a cat creeps toward a mirror at a rate of 0.20 m/s, at what speed will the cat and the cat's image approach each other?

Solution: In one second, the cat will be 0.20 meters closer to the mirror. At the same time, the cat's image will be 0.20 meters closer to the cat. Therefore, the cat and its image are approaching each other at the speed of 0.40 m/s. A characteristic of plane mirror images is that the object distance is equal to the image distance; i.e. the image is the same distance behind the mirror as the object is in front of the mirror.

Plane mirrors form virtual images. In other words, the image is formed behind the mirror where light does not actually reach. Another characteristic of plane mirrors is left-right reversal.

Example: Suppose you are standing in front of a mirror with your right hand raised. The image in the mirror will be raising its left hand.

Problem: If an object that is two feet tall is placed in front of a plane mirror, how tall will the image of the object be?

<u>Solution:</u> The image of the object will have the same dimensions as the actual object, in this case, a height of two feet. This is because the magnification of an image in a plane mirror is 1.

Curved mirrors

<u>Problem:</u> A concave mirror collects light from a star. If the light rays converge at 50 cm, what is the radius of curvature of the mirror?

<u>Solution:</u> The point at which the rays converge is known as the focal point. The focal length, in this case, 50 cm, is the distance from the focal point to the mirror. The radius of curvature is the distance from the vertex to the center of curvature. The vertex is the point on the mirror where the principal axis meets the mirror. The center of curvature represents the point in the center of the sphere from which the mirror was sliced. Since the focal point is the midpoint of the line from the vertex to the center of curvature, or focal length, the focal length would be one-half the radius of curvature. Since the focal length in this case is 50 cm, the radius of curvature would be 100 cm.

<u>Problem:</u> An image of an object in a mirror is upright and reduced in size. In what type of mirror is this image being viewed, plane, concave, or convex?

<u>Solution:</u> The image in a plane mirror would be the same size as the object. The image in a concave mirror would be magnified if upright. Only a convex mirror would produce a reduced upright image of an object.

Skill 6.6 Solve problems and analyze situations involving thin lenses.

A lens is a device that causes electromagnetic radiation to converge or diverge. The most familiar lenses are made of glass or plastic and designed to concentrate or disperse visible light. Two of the most important parameters for a lens are its thickness and it's focal length. Focal length is a measure of how strongly light is concentrated or dispersed by a lens. For a convex or converging lens, the focal length is the distance at which a beam of light will be focused to a single spot. Conversely, for a concave or diverging lens, the focal length is the distance to the point from which a beam appears to be diverging.

A thin lens in one in which focal length is much greater than lens thickness. For problems involving thin lenses, we can disregard any optical effects of the lens itself. Additionally, we can assume that the light that interacts with the lens makes a small angle with the optical axis of the system and so the sine and tangent values of the angle are approximately equal to the angle itself. This paraxial approximation, along with the thin lens assumptions, allows us to state:

$$\frac{1}{s} + \frac{1}{s'} = \frac{1}{f}$$

Where s=distance from the lens to the object (object location)
s'=distance from the lens to the image (image location)
f=focal length of the lens

Most lenses also cause some magnification of the object. Magnification is defined as:

$$m = \frac{y'}{y} = -\frac{s'}{s}$$

Where m=magnification
y'=image height
y=object height

The images produced by lenses can be either virtual or real. A virtual image is one that is created by rays of light that appear to diverge from a certain point. Virtual images cannot be seen on a screen because the light rays do not actually meet at the point where the image is located. If an image and object appear on the same side of a converging lens, that image is defined as virtual. For virtual images, the image location will be negative and the magnification positive. Real images, on the other hand, are formed by light rays actually passing through the image. Thus, real images are visible on a screen. Real images created by a converging lens are inverted and have a positive image location and negative magnification.

Sign conventions will make it easier to understand thin lens problems:

Focal length: positive for a converging lens; negative for a diverging lens
Object location: positive when in front of the lens; negative when behind the lens
Image location: positive when behind the lens; negative when in front of the lens
Image height: positive when upright; negative when upside-down.
Magnification: positive for an erect, virtual image; negative for an inverted, real image

Example:
A converging lens has a focal length of 10.00 cm and forms a 2.0 cm tall image of a 4.00 mm tall real object to the left of the lens. If the image is erect, is the image real or virtual? What are the locations of the object and the image?

Solution:

We begin by determining magnification:

$$m = \frac{y'}{y} = \frac{0.02m}{0.004m} = 5$$

Since the magnification is positive and the image is erect, we know the image must be virtual.

To find the locations of the object and image, we first relate them by using the magnification:

$$m = -\frac{s'}{s}$$
$$s' = -ms$$

Then we substitute into the thin lens equation, creating one variable in one unknown:

$$\frac{1}{s} + \frac{1}{s'} = \frac{1}{f}$$

$$\frac{1}{s} - \frac{1}{5s} = \frac{1}{10cm}$$

$$\frac{5-1}{5s} = \frac{1}{10cm}$$

$$s = \frac{40cm}{5} = 8cm \rightarrow \rightarrow s' = -5 \times 8cm = -40cm$$

Thus the object is located 8 cm to the left of the lens and the image is 40 cm to the left of the lens.

Skill 6.7 Solve problems and analyze situations involving patterns produced by diffraction and interference of light (e.g., single-slit, double-slit, diffraction gratings).

Diffraction is an important characteristic of waves. This occurs when part of a wave front is obstructed. Diffraction and interference are essentially the same physical process. Diffraction refers to various phenomena associated with wave propagation such as the bending, spreading, and interference of waves emerging from an aperture. It occurs with any type of wave including sound waves, water waves, and electromagnetic waves such as light and radio waves.

The effects of diffraction were first observed and characterized by Francesco Maria Grimaldi, who also gave the phenomenon the name diffraction. The research work of Grimaldi was published in 1665. Isaac Newton studied these effects and attributed them to inflexion of light rays. James Gregory (1638 – 1675) observed the diffraction patterns caused by a bird feather. In 1803, Thomas Young observed two-slit diffraction and concluded that light must travel as waves.

Here, we take a close look at important phenomena like single-slit diffraction, double-slit diffraction, diffraction grating, other forms of diffraction and lastly interference.

1. Single-slit diffraction: The simplest example of diffraction is single-slit diffraction in which the slit is narrow and a pattern of semi-circular ripples is formed after the wave passes through the slit.

2. Double-slit diffraction: These patterns are formed by the interference of light diffracting through two narrow slits.

3. Diffraction grating: Diffraction grating is a reflecting or transparent element whose optical properties are periodically modulated. In simple terms, diffraction gratings are fine parallel and equally spaced grooves or rulings on a material surface. When light is incident on a diffraction grating, light is reflected or transmitted in discrete directions, called diffraction orders. Because of their light dispersive properties, gratings are commonly used in monochromators and spectrophotometers. Gratings are usually designated by their groove density, expressed in grooves/millimeter. A fundamental property of gratings is that the angle of deviation of all but one of the diffracted beams depends on the wavelength of the incident light.

4. Other forms of diffraction:

i) Particle diffraction: It is the diffraction of particles such as electrons, which is used as a powerful argument for quantum theory. It is possible to observe the diffraction of particles such as neutrons or electrons and hence we are able to infer the existence of wave particle duality.

ii) Bragg diffraction: This is diffraction from a multiple slits, and is similar to what occurs when waves are scattered from a periodic structure such as atoms in a crystal or rulings on a diffraction grating. Bragg diffraction is used in X-ray crystallography to deduce the structure of a crystal from the angles at which the X-rays are diffracted from it.

5. Interference: Interference is described as the superposition of two or more waves resulting in a new wave pattern. Interference is involved in Thomas Young's double slit experiment where two beams of light which are coherent with each other interfere to produce an interference pattern. Light from any source can be used to obtain interference patterns. For example, Newton's rings can be produced with sun light. However, in general, white light is less suited for producing clear interference patterns as it is a mix of a full spectrum of colors. Sodium light is close to monochromatic and is thus more suitable for producing interference patterns. The most suitable is laser light as it is almost perfectly monochromatic.

Problem: The interference maxima (location of bright spots created by constructive interference) for double-slit interference are given by

$$\frac{n\lambda}{d} = \frac{x}{D} = \sin\theta \quad n=1,2,3\ldots$$

where λ is the wavelength of the light, d is the distance between the two slits, D is the distance between the slits and the screen on which the pattern is observed and x is the location of the nth maximum. If the two slits are 0.1mm apart, the screen is 5m away from the slits, and the first maximum beyond the center one is 2.0 cm from the center of the screen, what is the wavelength of the light?

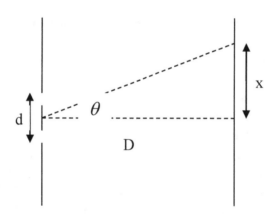

Solution: λ = xd/(Dn) = 0.02 x 0.0001/ (5 x1) = 400 nanometers

Skill 6.8   Identify the use and characteristics of various optical instruments (e.g., eye, spectroscope, camera, telescope, microscope, corrective lenses).

Eye

The eye is a very complex sensory organ. Although there are many critical anatomical features of the eye, the lens and retina are the most important for focusing and sensing light. Light passes through the cornea and through the lens. The lens is attached to numerous muscles that contract and relax to move the lens in order to focus the light onto the retina. The pupil also contracts and relaxes to allow more or less light in the eye as required.

The retina contains rod cells which are responsible for vision in low light and cone cells which sense color and detail. Different types of cone cells are capable of sensing different wavelengths of light. A chemical called rhodopsin is present in the retina that converts light signals into electrical impulses that are sent to the brain to interpret as vision. The retina is lined with a black pigment called melanin that reduces reflection.

The eye relies on refraction to focus light onto the retina. Refraction occurs at four curved interfaces; between the air and the front of the cornea, the back of the cornea and the aqueous humor, the aqueous humor at the front of the lens, and the back of the lens and the vitreous humor. When each of these interfaces are working properly the light arrives at the retina in perfect focus for transmission to the brain as an image.

Eye Glasses

When all the parts of the eye are not working together correctly, corrective lenses or eyeglasses may be needed to assist the eye in focusing the light onto the retina. The surfaces of the lens or cornea may not be smooth causing the light to refract in the wrong direction. This is called astigmatism. Another common problem is that the lens is not able to change its curvature appropriately to match the image. The cornea can also be misshaped resulting in blurred vision. Corrective lenses consist of curves pieces of glass which bend the light in order to change the focal point of the light. A nearsighted eye forms images in front of the retina. To correct this, a minus lens consisting of two concave prisms is used to bend light out and move the image back to the retina. A farsighted eye creates images behind the retina. This is corrected using plus lenses that bend light in and bring the image forward onto the retina. The worse the vision, the farther out of focus the image is on the retina. Therefore the stronger the lens the further the focal point is moved to compensate.

Spectroscope

Spectrometers known as spectroscopes are used to identify materials. Spectroscopes are used often in astronomy and some branches of chemistry. Early spectroscopes were simply a prism with graduations marking wavelengths of light. Modern spectroscopes typically use a diffraction grating, a movable slit, and some kind of photo detector, all automated and controlled by a computer. When materials are heated they emit light that is characteristic of its atomic composition. The emission of certain frequencies of light produce a pattern of lines that are comparable to a fingerprint. The yellow light emission of heated sodium is a typical example.

A spectroscope is able to detect, measure and record the frequencies of the emitted light. This is done by passing the light though a slit to a collimating lens which transforms the light into parallel rays. The light is then passed through a prism that refracts the beam into a spectrum of different wavelengths. The image is then viewed alongside a scale to determine the characteristic wavelengths. Spectral analysis is an important tool for determining and analyzing the composition of unknown materials as well as for astronomical studies.

Camera

A camera is another device that utilizes the lens' ability to refract light to capture and process an image. As with the eye, light enters the lens of a camera and focuses the light on the other side. Instead of focusing on the retina, the image is focused on the film to create a film negative. This film negative is later processed with chemicals to create a photograph. A camera uses a converging or convex lens. This lens captures and directs light to a single point to create a real image on the surface of the film. To focus a camera on an image, the distance of the lens from the film is adjusted in order to ensure that the real image converges on the surface of the film and not in front of or behind it.

Different lenses are available which capture and bend the light to different degrees. A lens with more pronounced curvature will be able to bend the light more acutely causing the image to converge more closely to the lens. Conversely a flatter lens will have a longer focal distance. The further the lens is located from the film (flatter lens), the larger the image becomes. Thus zoom lenses on cameras are flat while wide angle lenses are more rounded. The focal length number on a certain lens conveys the magnification ability of the lens.

The film functions like the retina of the eye in that it is light sensitive and can capture light images when exposed. However, this exposure must be brief to capture the contrasting amounts of light and a clear image. The rest of the camera functions to precisely control how much light contacts the film. The aperture is the lens opening which can open and close to let in more or less light. The temporal length of light exposure is controlled by the shutter which can be set at different speeds depending on the amount of action and level of light available. The film speed refers to the size of the light sensitive grains on the surface of the film. The larger grains absorb more light photons than the smaller grains, so film speed should be selected according to lighting conditions.

Telescope

A telescope is a device that has the ability to make distant objects appear to be much closer. Most telescopes are one of two varieties, a refractor which uses lenses or a reflector which uses mirrors. Each accomplishes the same purpose but in totally different ways. The basic idea of a telescope is to collect as much light as possible, focus it, and then magnify it. The objective lens or primary mirror of a telescope brings the light from an object into focus. An eyepiece lens takes the focused light and "spreads it out" or magnifies it using the same principle as a magnifying glass using two curved surfaces to refract the light.

Microscope

Microscopes are used to view objects that are too small to be seen with the naked eye. A microscope usually has an objective lens that collects light from the sample and an eyepiece which brings the image into focus for the observer. It also has a light source to illuminate the sample. Typical optical microscopes achieve magnification of up to 1500 times.

Skill 6.9   Interpret the relationship between light intensity and distance from source (inverse square law).

For all physical quantities, intensity is a measure of flux over time (see Section VII-2 for a discussion of flux). Light intensity is sometimes referred to as irradiance, radiant emittance, or radiant exitance. The following is the mathematical relationship between intensity and power.

$$I \; \alpha \; \frac{P}{r^2}$$

Where I=intensity
P=power
r=distance from light source

Note that intensity is inversely proportional to squared distance from the source. This means there is a steep drop off of light intensity as one moves away from the light source. For instance, if the distance between a light source and an observer is doubled, the intensity is decreased to $(1/2)^2$ = 1/4 of its original value.

The inverse square law may be understood from purely geometric considerations. Since the light from a point source radiates uniformly in all directions, at a distance r from the source the power is distributed over a sphere with radius r and area proportional to r squared.

Skill 6.10 Relate and analyze various ranges of electromagnetic spectrum.

The electromagnetic spectrum is measured using frequency (f) in hertz or wavelength (λ) in meters. The frequency times the wavelength of every electromagnetic wave equals the speed of light (3.0×10^8 meters/second).

Roughly, the range of wavelengths of the electromagnetic spectrum is:

	f	**λ**
Radio waves	$10^5 - 10^{-1}$ hertz	$10^3 - 10^9$ meters
Microwaves	$3 \times 10^9 - 3 \times 10^{11}$ hertz	$10^{-3} - 10^{-1}$ meters
Infrared radiation	$3 \times 10^{11} - 4 \times 10^{14}$ hertz	$7 \times 10^{-7} - 10^{-3}$ meters
Visible light	$4 \times 10^{14} - 7.5 \times 10^{14}$ hertz	$4 \times 10^{-7} - 7 \times 10^{-7}$ meters
Ultraviolet radiation	$7.5 \times 10^{14} - 3 \times 10^{16}$ hertz	$10^{-8} - 4 \times 10^{-7}$ meters
X-Rays	$3 \times 10^{16} - 3 \times 10^{19}$ hertz	$10^{-11} - 10^{-8}$ meters
Gamma Rays	$> 3 \times 10^{19}$ hertz	$< 10^{-11}$ meters

Radio waves are used for transmitting data. Common examples are television, cell phones, and wireless computer networks. Microwaves are used to heat food and deliver Wi-Fi service. Infrared waves are utilized in night vision goggles. Visible light we are all familiar with as the human eye is most sensitive to this wavelength range. UV light causes sunburns and would be even more harmful if most of it were not captured in the Earth's ozone layer. X-rays aid us in the medical field and gamma rays are most useful in the field of astronomy.

COMPETENCY VII.   KNOWLEDGE OF ELECTRICITY AND MAGNETISM

Skill 7.1   Calculate the force on a point charge due to one or more other charges.

Any point charge may experience force resulting from attraction to or repulsion from another charged object. The easiest way to begin analyzing this phenomenon and calculating this force is by considering two point charges. Let us say that the charge on the first point is Q_1, the charge on the second point is Q_2, and the distance between them is r. Their interaction is governed by Coulomb's Law which gives the formula for the force F as:

$$F = k \frac{Q_1 Q_2}{r^2}$$

where k= $9.0 \times 10^9 \, \dfrac{N \cdot m^2}{C^2}$ (known as Coulomb's constant)

The charge is a scalar quantity, however, the force has direction. For two point charges, the direction of the force is along a line joining the two charges. Note that the force will be repulsive if the two charges are both positive or both negative and attractive if one charge is positive and the other negative. Thus, a negative force indicates an attractive force.

When more than one point charge is exerting force on a point charge, we simply apply Coulomb's Law multiple times and then combine the forces as we would in any statics problem. Let's examine the process in the following example problem.

<u>Problem:</u> Three point charges are located at the vertices of a right triangle as shown below. Charges, angles, and distances are provided (drawing not to scale). Find the force exerted on the point charge A.

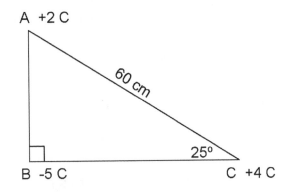

Solution: First we find the individual forces exerted on A by point B and point C. We have the information we need to find the magnitude of the force exerted on A by C.

$$F_{AC} = k\frac{Q_1 Q_2}{r^2} = 9\times10^9\ \frac{N\cdot m^2}{C^2}\left(\frac{4C\times 2C}{(0.6m)^2}\right) = 2\times10^{11}N$$

To determine the magnitude of the force exerted on A by B, we must first determine the distance between them.

$$\sin 25° = \frac{r_{AB}}{60cm}$$
$$r_{AB} = 60cm\times\sin 25° = 25cm$$

Now we can determine the force.

$$F_{AB} = k\frac{Q_1 Q_2}{r^2} = 9\times10^9\ \frac{N\cdot m^2}{C^2}\left(\frac{-5C\times 2C}{(0.25m)^2}\right) = -1.4\times10^{12}N$$

We can see that there is an attraction in the direction of B (negative force) and repulsion in the direction of C (positive force). To find the net force, we must consider the direction of these forces (along the line connecting any two point charges). We add them together using the law of cosines.

$$F_A^{\ 2} = F_{AB}^{\ 2} + F_{AC}^{\ 2} - 2F_{AB}F_{AC}\cos 75°$$
$$F_A^{\ 2} = (-1.4\times10^{12}N)^2 + (2\times10^{11}N)^2 - 2(-1.4\times10^{12}N)(2\times10^{11}N)^2\cos 75°$$
$$F_A = 1.5\times10^{12}N$$

This gives us the magnitude of the net force, now we will find its direction using the law of sines.
$$\frac{\sin\theta}{F_{AC}} = \frac{\sin 75°}{F_A}$$
$$\sin\theta = F_{AC}\frac{\sin 75°}{F_A} = 2\times10^{11}N\frac{\sin 75°}{1.5\times10^{12}N}$$
$$\theta = 7.3°$$

Thus, the net force on A is 7.3° west of south and has magnitude 1.5 x 10¹²N. Looking back at our diagram, this makes sense, because A should be attracted to B (pulled straight south) but the repulsion away from C "pushes" this force in a westward direction.

Skill 7.2 Calculate the electrical potential difference between two locations within an electric field.

An electric field exists in the space surrounding a charge. Electric fields have both direction and magnitude determined by the strength and direction in which they exhibit force on a test charge. The units used to measure electric fields are newtons per coulomb (N/C). Electric potential is simply the potential energy per unit of charge. Given this definition, it is clear that electric potential must be measured in joules per coulomb and this unit is known as a volt (J/C=V).

Within an electric field there are typically differences in potential energy. This difference may be referred to as voltage. The difference in electrical potential between two points is the amount of work needed to move a unit charge from the first point to the second point. Stated mathematically, this is:

$$V = \frac{W}{Q}$$

where V= the potential difference
W= the work done to move the charge
Q= the charge

We know from mechanics, however, that work is simply force applied over a certain distance. We can combine this with Coulomb's law to find the work done between two charges distance r apart.

$$W = F.r = k\frac{Q_1 Q_2}{r^2}.r = k\frac{Q_1 Q_2}{r}$$

Now we can simply substitute this back into the equation above for electric potential:

$$V_2 = \frac{W}{Q_2} = \frac{k\dfrac{Q_1 Q_2}{r}}{Q_2} = k\frac{Q_1}{r}$$

Let's examine a sample problem involving electrical potential.
Problem: What is the electric potential at point A due to the 2 shown charges? If a charge of +2.0 C were infinitely far away, how much work would be required to bring it to point A?

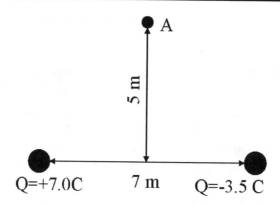

Solution: To determine the electric potential at point A, we simple find and add the potential from the two charges (this is the principle of superposition). From the diagram, we can assume that A is equidistant from each charge. Using the Pythagorean theorem, we determine this distance to be 6.1 m.

$$V = \frac{kq}{r} = k\left(\frac{7.0C}{6.1m} + \frac{-3.5C}{6.1m}\right) = 9 \times 10^9 \frac{N.m^2}{C^2}\left(0.57\frac{C}{m}\right) = 5.13 \times 10^9 V$$

Now, let's consider bringing the charged particle to point A. We assume that electric potential of these particle is initially zero because it is infinitely far away. Since now know the potential at point A, we can calculate the work necessary to bring the particle from V=0:

$$W = VQ = (5.13 \times 10^9) \times 2J = 10.26 \times 10^9 J$$

The large results for potential and work make it apparent how large the unit coloumb is. For this reason, most problems deal in microcoulombs (μC).

Skill 7.3 Solve and analyze problems involving capacitance, with or without dielectrics.

Capacitance (C) is a measure of the stored electric charge per unit electric potential. The mathematical definition is:

$$C = \frac{Q}{V}$$

It follows from the definition above that the units of capacitance are coulombs per volt, a unit known as a farad ($F=C/V$). In circuits, devices called parallel plate capacitors are formed by two closely spaced conductors. The function of capacitors is to store electrical energy. When a voltage is applied, electrical charges build up in both the conductors (typically referred to as plates). These charges on the two plates have equal magnitude but opposite sign. The capacitance of a capacitor is a function of the distance d between the two plates and the area A of the plates:

$$C \approx \frac{\varepsilon A}{d}; A \gg d^2$$

Capacitance also depends on the permittivity of the non-conducting matter between the plates of the capacitor. This matter may be only air or almost any other non-conducting material and is referred to as a dielectric. The permittivity of empty space ε_0 is roughly equivalent to that for air, ε_{air}=8.854x10^{-12} C ^{2}/N•m^2. For other materials, the dielectric constant, κ, is the permittivity of the material in relation to air ($\kappa=\varepsilon/\varepsilon_{air}$). The make-up of the dielectric is critical to the capacitor's function because it determines the maximum energy that can be stored by the capacitor. This is because an overly strong electric field will eventually destroy the dielectric.

In summary, a capacitor is "charged" as electrical energy is delivered to it and opposite charges accumulate on the two plates. The two plates generate electric fields and a voltage develops across the dielectric. The energy stored in the capacitor, then, is equal to the amount of work necessary to create this voltage. The mathematical statement of this is:

$$E_{stored} = \frac{1}{2}CV^2 = \frac{1}{2}\frac{Q^2}{C} = \frac{1}{2}VQ$$

Problem: Imagine that a parallel plate capacitor has an area of 10.00 cm ^{2} and a capacitance of 4.50 pF. The capacitor is connected to a 12.0 V battery. The capacitor is completely charged and then the battery is removed. What is the separation of the plates in the capacitor? How much energy is stored between the plates? We've assumed that this capacitor initially had no dielectric (i.e., only air between the plates) but now imagine it has a Mylar dielectric that fully fills the space. What will the new capacitance be? (for Mylar, $\kappa=3.5$)

Solution: To determine the separation of the plates, we use our equation for a capacitor:

$$C = \frac{\varepsilon_0 A}{d}$$

We can simply solve for d and plug in our values:

$$d = \varepsilon_0 \frac{A}{C} = \left(8.854 \times 10^{-12} \frac{C}{N \cdot m^2}\right) \frac{10 \times 10^{-4} m^2}{4.5 \times 10^{-12} F} = 1.97 \times 10^{-3} m = 1.97 mm$$

Similarly, to find stored energy, we simply employ the equation above:

$$E_{stored} = \frac{1}{2} QV$$

But we don't yet know the charge Q, so we must first find it from the definition of capacitance:

$$C = \frac{Q}{V}$$

$$Q = CV = (4.5 \times 10^{-12}) \times (12V) = 5.4 \times 10^{-11} C$$

Now we can find the stored energy:

$$E_{stored} = \frac{1}{2} QV = \frac{1}{2}(5.4 \times 10^{-11} C)(12V) = 3.24 \times 10^{-10} J$$

To find the capacitance with a Mylar dielectric, we again use the equation for capacitance of a parallel plate capacitor. Note that the new capacitance can be found by multiplying the original capacitance by κ:

$$C = \frac{\kappa_{Mylar} \varepsilon_0 A}{d} = \kappa_{Mylar} C_0 = 3.5 \times 4.5 pF = 15.75 pF$$

Skill 7.4 Analyze electric fields due to charge configuration.

Electric fields can be generated by a single point charge or by a collection of charges in close proximity. The electric field generated from a point charge is given by:

$$E = \frac{kQ}{r^2}$$

where E= the electric field

k= $9.0 \times 10^9 \, \dfrac{N \cdot m^2}{C^2}$ (Coulomb's constant)

Q= the point charge
r= distance from the charge

Electric fields are visualized with field lines, which demonstrate the strength and direction of an electric field. The electric field around a positive charge points away from the charge and the electric field around a negative charge points toward the charge.

While it's easy enough to calculate and visualize the field generated by a single point charge, we can also determine the nature of an electric field produced by a collection of charge simply by adding the vectors from the individual charges. This is known as the superposition principle (superposition of force and potential were shown in the sample problems in Sections VII-1 and 2). The following equation demonstrates how this principle can be used to determine the field resulting from hundreds or thousands of charges.

$$\vec{E}_{total} = \sum_i \vec{E}_i = \vec{E}_1 + \vec{E}_2 + \vec{E}_3 \ldots$$

Skill 7.5   Analyze electric fields in terms of electric flux and Gauss' law.

In any physical phenomenon, flux refers to rate of movement of a substance or energy through a certain area. Flux can be used to quantify the movement of mass, heat, momentum, light, molecules and other things. Flux depends on density of flow, area, and direction of the flow. To visualize this, imagine a kitchen sieve under a tap of flowing water. The water that passes through the sieve is the flux; the flux will decrease if we lower the water flow rate, decrease the size of the sieve, or tilt the sieve away from direction of the water's flow. Electric flux, then, is just the number of electric field lines that pass through a given area. It is given by the following equation:

$$\Phi = E(\cos\phi)A$$

where Φ = flux
E = the electric field
A = area
ϕ = the angle between the electric field and a vector normal to the surface A

Thus, if a plane is parallel to an electric field, no field lines will pass through that plane and the flux through it will be zero. If a plane is perpendicular to an electric field, the flux through it will be maximal.

Gauss's Law says that the electric flux through a surface is equal to the charge enclosed by a surface divided by a constant ε_0 (permittivity of free space). The simplest mathematical statement of this law is:

$$\Phi = Q_A / \varepsilon_0$$

where Q_A = the charge enclosed by the surface

Gauss's Law provides us with a useful and powerful method to calculate electric fields. For instance, imagine a solid conducting sphere with a net charge Q_s. We know from Gauss's Law that the electric field inside the sphere must be zero and all the excess charge lies on the outer surface of the sphere. The field produced by this sphere is the same a point charge of value Q_s. This conclusion is true whether the sphere is solid or hollow.

Skill 7.6 Analyze charge distribution problems involving various shaped conductors and nonconductors.

Electrical conduction is the movement of charged particles (electrons) through a medium. Those materials that allow for free and easy movement of electrons are called conductors. Some of the best conductors are metal, especially copper and silver. Materials that do not allow conduction are call insulators. Good insulators include, glass, rubber, and wood. Materials with intermediate conduction properties are known as semi-conductors and are useful in situations where controlled conduction is required.

When charge is transferred to a mass of a material, the response is highly dependent on whether that material is a conductor or insulator. In a conductor, the electrons will flow freely and the charge will quickly distribute itself across the material. In an insulator, however, the movement of electrons will be highly impeded and so the charge will remain localized at the point where it was introduced.

Within conducting materials, the shape of the mass also has an effect. If the surface of a conductor is uniform, so will the charge distribution be. For example, if we had a sphere or a thin sheet of copper and we introduced a charge at one point, that charge would be uniformly spread across the surface of the copper. However, charge will not be uniform if the surfaces are different. Specifically, more charge accumulates on a surface with a shorter radius of curvature than on a surface with a longer one. For instance, if we had a tear-dropped shape of copper, the "point" of the tear-drop would have higher charge than the spherical region of the tear-drop.

Skill 7.7   Simplify series and parallel combinations of resistors or capacitors.

Capacitors were introduced in Section VII-3.

Resistors are electrical devices that oppose electrical currents and create a voltage drop as specified by Ohm's Law (Section VII-8). The units for electrical resistance are ohms.

Often resistors and capacitors are used together in series or parallel. Two components are in series if one end of the first element is connected to one end of the second component. The components are in parallel if both ends of one element are connected to the corresponding ends of another. A series circuit has a single path for current flow through all of its elements. A parallel circuit is one that requires more than one path for current flow in order to reach all of the circuit elements. Below is a diagram demonstrating a simple circuit with resistors in parallel (on right) and in series (on left). Note the symbols used for a battery (noted V) and the resistors (noted R).

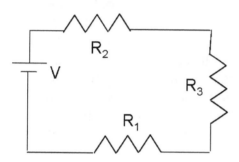 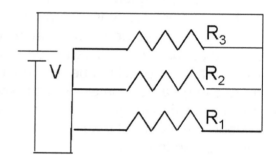

Thus, when the resistors are placed in series, the current through each one will be the same. When they are placed in parallel, the voltage through each one will be the same. To understand basic circuitry, it is important to master the rules by which the equivalent resistance (R_{eq}) or capacitance (C_{eq}) can be calculated from a number of resistors or capacitors:

Resistors in parallel:
$$\frac{1}{R_{eq}} = \frac{1}{R_1} + \frac{1}{R_2} + \cdots + \frac{1}{R_n}$$

Resistors in series: $R_{eq} = R_1 + R_2 + \cdots + R_n$

Capacitors in parallel: $C_{eq} = C_1 + C_2 + \cdots + C_n$

Capacitors in series:
$$\frac{1}{C_{eq}} = \frac{1}{C_1} + \frac{1}{C_2} + \cdots + \frac{1}{C_n}$$

Skill 7.8 Solve and analyze problems using Ohm's law.

Ohm's Law is the most important tool we posses to analyze electrical circuits. Ohm's Law states that the current passing through a conductor is directly proportional to the voltage drop and inversely proportional to the resistance of the conductor. Stated mathematically, this is:

$$V = IR$$

Problem:
The circuit diagram at right shows three resistors connected to a battery in series. A current of 1.0A flows through the circuit in the direction shown. It is known that the equivalent resistance of this circuit is 25 Ω. What is the total voltage supplied by the battery?

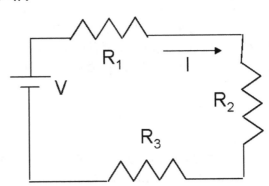

Solution:

To determine the battery's voltage, we simply apply Ohm's Law:

$$V = IR = 1.0A \times 25\Omega = 25V$$

Skill 7.9 Apply Kirchoff's laws to analysis of loop DC circuits.

Kirchoff's Laws are a pair of laws that apply to conservation of charge and energy in circuits and were developed by Gustav Kirchoff.

Kirchoff's Current Law: At any point in a circuit where charge density is constant, the sum of currents flowing toward the point must be equal to the sum of currents flowing away from that point.

Kirchoff's Voltage Law: The sum of the electrical potential differences around a circuit must be zero.

While these statements may seem rather simple, they can be very useful in analyzing DC circuits, those involving constant circuit voltages and currents.

Problem:
The circuit diagram at right shows three resistors connected to a battery in series. A current of 1.0 A is generated by the battery. The potential drop across R_1, R_2, and R_3 are 5V, 6V, and 10V. What is the total voltage supplied by the battery?

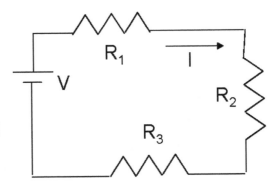

Solution:
Kirchoff's Voltage Law tells us that the total voltage supplied by the battery must be equal to the total voltage drop across the circuit. Therefore:

$$V_{battery} = V_{R_1} + V_{R_2} + V_{R_3} = 5V + 6V + 10V = 21V$$

Problem:
The circuit diagram at right shows three resistors wired in parallel with a 12V battery. The resistances of R_1, R_2, and R_3 are 4 Ω, 5 Ω, and 6 Ω, respectively. What is the total current?

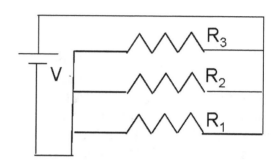

Solution:
This is a more complicated problem. Because the resistors are wired in parallel, we know that the voltage entering each resistor must be the same and equal to that supplied by the battery. We can combine this knowledge with Ohm's Law to determine the current across each resistor:

$$I_1 = \frac{V_1}{R_1} = \frac{12V}{4\Omega} = 3A$$

$$I_2 = \frac{V_2}{R_2} = \frac{12V}{5\Omega} = 2.4A$$

$$I_3 = \frac{V_3}{R_3} = \frac{12V}{6\Omega} = 2A$$

Finally, we use Kirchoff's Current Law to find the total current:

$$I = I_1 + I_2 + I_3 = 3A + 2.4A + 2A = 7.4A$$

Skill 7.10 Calculate and analyze the power produced by or dissipated through a given DC circuit element.

Electrical power is a measure of how much work can be done by an electrical current and has units of watts (W). To determine electrical power, we simply use Joule's law:

$$P = IV$$

where P=power
I=current
V=voltage

If we combine this with Ohm's law (V=IR), we generate two new equations that are useful for finding the amount of power dissipated by a resistor:

$$P = I^2 R$$

$$P = \frac{V^2}{R}$$

Problem: How much power is dissipated by a 1 kΩ resistor with a 50V voltage drop through it?

Solution:

$$P = \frac{V^2}{R} = \frac{(50V)^2}{1000\Omega} = 2.5W$$

Skill 7.11 Analyze and compare power dissipated in various configurations of battery-light bulb circuits (e.g., ranking brightness, change in brightness).

Typical incandescent light bulbs contain tungsten filaments through which a current flows. The filament dissipates this current in the form of heat and light. Light bulbs behave similarly to other resistors when they are placed in series or in parallel. Thus, when the light bulbs are placed in series in a simple circuit with a battery, the total circuit voltage will be distributed over each resistor and the current through each will be the total current. When they are placed in parallel, the voltage across each bulb will be the total voltage while the total current is distributed between the different branches. The key factor that determines the brightness of the bulbs is the total resistance of the circuit. When n light bulbs, each of resistance R, are placed in series, the total resistance of the circuit is nR. For n light bulbs in parallel, however, the total resistance is R/n and actually falls as the number of light bulbs is increased.

If light bulbs are in parallel, they will all be equally bright because the same amount of current flows through each bulb (assuming the bulbs are identical and have the same resistance). When more light bulbs are added in parallel, the brightness of each light bulb will remain unchanged since the overall resistance of the circuit is less and more current flows through the circuit providing the additional current needed for the new light bulbs. Since each light bulb is in its own branch, removing one does not affect current flow through the other branches. The appliances in a house are wired in parallel and run independently of each other.

Light bulbs wired in series are also equally bright since the same current flows through each of them but they are less bright than the same number of light bulbs wired in parallel since the circuit resistance is greater. When more light bulbs are added in series, the brightness of each bulb decreases since current flow is reduced due to increased circuit resistance. Removing one of the bulbs causes a break in the circuit and immediately puts out the other bulbs. Needless to say, electrical appliances in a home are not wired in series.

Skill 7.12 Solve and analyze problems involving resistance of a conductor using resistivity and temperature information.

Conductors are those materials which allow for the free passage of electrical current. However, all materials exhibit a certain opposition to the movement of electrons. This opposition is known as resistivity (ρ). Resistivity is determined experimentally by measuring the resistance of a uniformly shaped sample of the material and applying the following equation:

$$\rho = R\frac{A}{l}$$

where ρ = static resistivity of the material
R = electrical resistance of the material sample
A = cross-sectional area of the material sample
L = length of the material sample

The temperature at which these measurements are taken is important as it has been shown that resistivity is a function of temperature. For conductors, resistivity increases with increasing temperature and decreases with decreasing temperature. At extremely low temperatures resistivity assumes a low and constant value known as residual resistivity ($\rho 0$). Residual resistivity is a function of the type and purity of the conductor.

The following equation allows us to calculate the resistivity ρ of a material at any temperature given the resistivity at a reference temperature, in this case at $20^{0}C$:

$$\rho = \rho_{20}[1 + a(t - 20)]$$

where ρ_{20} = resistivity at $20^{0}C$
a= proportionality constant characteristic of the material
t=temperature in Celcius

Problem: The tungsten filament in a certain light bulb is a wire 8 μm in diameter and 10 mm long. Given that, for tungsten, $\rho_{20} = 5.5 \times 10^{-8}$ $\Omega\cdot$m and $a = 4.5 \times 10^{-3} K^{-1}$, what will the resistance of the filament be at 45°C?

Solution: First we must find the resistivity of the tungsten at 45°C:

$$\rho = 5.5 \times 10^{-8}\left(1 + 4.5 \times 10^{-3}(45 - 20)\right) = 6.1 \times 10^{-8}\Omega.m$$

Now we can rearrange the equation defining resistivity and solve for the resistance of the filament:

$$R = \rho\frac{l}{A} = 6.1 \times 10^{-8} \times 0.01 / (\pi(4 \times 10^{-6})^{2}) = 12.1\Omega$$

Skill 7.13 Analyze the patterns of magnetic field lines in the presence of one or more permanent magnets.

Magnetic field lines are a good way to visualize a magnetic field. The distance between magnetic fields lines indicates the strength of the magnetic field such that the lines are closer together near the poles of the magnets where the magnetic field is the strongest. The lines spread out above and below the middle of the magnet, as the field is weakest at those points furthest from the two poles. The SI unit for magnetic field known as magnetic induction is Tesla(T) given by 1T = 1 N.s/(C.m) = 1 N/(A.m). Magnetic fields are often expressed in the smaller unit Gauss (G) (1 T = 10,000 G). Magnetic field lines always point from the north pole of a magnet to the south pole.

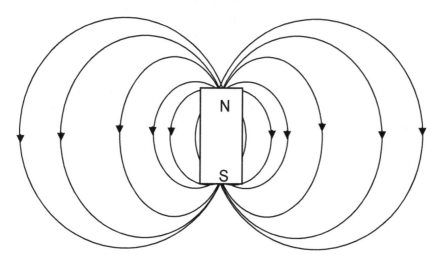

Magnetic field lines can be plotted with a magnetized needle that is free to turn in 3 dimensions. Usually a compass needle is used in demonstrations. The direction tangent to the magnetic field line is the direction the compass needle will point in a magnetic field. Iron filings spread on a flat surface or magnetic field viewing film which contains a slurry of iron filings are another way to see magnetic field lines.

When two magnets are placed close to one another magnetic field lines form between the north and south pole of each magnet individually and the field line also interact between the two magnets. The magnetic field in the area between the two magnets will depend on how the magnets are oriented with respect to one another. If the north pole of one magnet is placed near the south pole of the other magnet, for instance, you can see field lines starting at that north pole and ending at the south pole of the other magnet. If additional magnets and metal objects are placed in the arrangement the interactions become more complicated and various patterns are formed by the magnetic field lines.

Skill 7.14 Solve and analyze problems involving the direction and magnitude of the magnetic force acting on moving charges (e.g., mass spectrometer).

The magnetic force exerted on a charge moving in a magnetic field depends on the size and velocity of the charge as well as the magnitude of the magnetic field. One important fact to remember is that only the velocity of the charge in a direction perpendicular to the magnetic field will affect the force exerted. Therefore, a charge moving parallel to the magnetic field will have no force acting upon it whereas a charge will feel the greatest force when moving perpendicular to the magnetic field.

The direction of the magnetic force is always at a right angle to the plane formed by the velocity vector v and the magnetic field B and is given by applying the right hand rule - if the fingers of the right hand are curled in a way that seems to rotate the v vector into the B vector, the thumb points in the direction of the force. The magnitude of the force is equal to the cross product of the velocity of the charge with the magnetic field multiplied by the magnitude of the charge.

$$F = q\,(v \times B) \quad or \quad F = q\,v\,B\sin(\theta)$$
Where θ is the angle formed between the vectors of velocity of the charge and direction of magnetic field.

Problem: Assuming we have a particle of 1×10^{-6} kg that has a charge of -8 coulombs that is moving perpendicular to a magnetic field in a clockwise direction on a circular path with a radius of 2 m and a speed of 2000 m/s, let's determine the magnitude and direction of the magnetic field acting upon it.
Solution: We know the mass, charge, speed, and path radius of the charged particle. Combining the equation above with the equation for centripetal force we get

$$qvB = \frac{mv^2}{r} \quad or \quad B = \frac{mv}{qr}$$

Thus B= $(1 \times 10^{-6}$ kg$)$ $(2000$m/s$)$ / $(-8$ C$)(2$ m$)$ = 1.25×10^{-4} Tesla

Since the particle is moving in a clockwise direction, we use the right hand rule and point our fingers clockwise along a circular path in the plane of the paper while pointing the thumb towards the center in the direction of the centripetal force. This requires the fingers to curl in a way that indicates that the magnetic field is pointing out of the page. However, since the particle has a negative charge we must reverse the final direction of the magnetic field into the page.

A mass spectrometer measures the mass to charge ratio of ions using a setup similar to the one described above. m/q is determined by measuring the path radius of particles of known velocity moving in a known magnetic field.

Skill 7.15 Calculate and analyze the electromagnetic force (emf) induced in a circuit when there is a change in the magnetic flux through the circuit.

When the magnetic flux through a coil is changed, a voltage is produced which is known as induced electromagnetic force. Magnetic flux is a term used to describe the number of magnetic fields lines that pass through an area and is described by the equation:

$$\Phi = B\ A\ \cos\theta$$

Where Φ is the angle between the magnetic field B, and the normal to the plane of the coil of area A

By changing any of these three inputs, magnetic field, area of coil, or angle between field and coil, the flux will change and an EMF can be induced. The speed at which these changes occur also affects the magnitude of the EMF, as a more rapid transition generates more EMF than a gradual one. This is described by **Faraday's law** of induction:

$$\varepsilon = -N\ \Delta\Phi\ /\ \Delta t$$

where ε is emf induced, N is the number of loops in a coil, t is time, and Φ is magnetic flux

The negative sign signifies **Lenz's law** which states that induced emf in a coil acts to oppose any change in magnetic flux. Thus the current flows in a way that creates a magnetic field in the direction opposing the change in flux. The right hand rule for this is that if your fingers curl in the direction of the induced current, your thumb points in the direction of the magnetic field it produces through the loop.

Consider a coil lying flat on the page with a square cross section that is 10 cm by 5 cm. The coil consists of 10 loops and has a magnetic field of 0.5 T passing through it coming out of the page. Let's find the induced EMF when the magnetic field is changed to 0.8 T in 2 seconds.

First, let's find the initial magnetic flux: Φ_i

$\Phi_i = BA \cos\theta = (.5\ T)\ (.05\ m)\ (.1m) \cos 0° = 0.0025\ T\ m^2$

And the final magnetic flux: Φ_f

$\Phi f = BA \cos\theta = (0.8\ T)\ (.05\ m)\ (.1m) \cos 0° = 0.004\ T\ m^2$

The induced emf is calculated then by

$\varepsilon = -N\ \Delta\Phi\ /\ \Delta t = -\ 10\ (.004\ T\ m^2 - .0025\ T\ m^2)\ /\ 2\ s = -0.0075$ volts.

To determine the direction the current flows in the coil we need to apply the right hand rule and Lenz's law. The magnetic flux is being increased out of the page, with your thumb pointing up the fingers are coiling counterclockwise. However, Lenz's law tells us the current will oppose the change in flux so the current in the coil will be flowing clockwise.

Skill 7.16 Apply concepts and solve problems involving transformers.

A transformer is a device that magnetically couples two circuits together. This allows the transfer of energy between these two circuits without requiring motion. Typically, a transformer consists of a couple of coils and a magnetic core. A changing voltage applied to one coil (the primary) creates a flux in the magnetic core, which induces voltage in the other coil (the secondary). All transformers operate on this simple principle though they range in size and function from those in tiny microphones to those that connect the components of the US power grid.

One of the most important functions of transformers is that they allow us to "step-up" and "step-down" between vastly different voltages. To determine how the voltage is changed by a transformer, we employ any of the following relationships:

$$\frac{V_s}{V_p} = \frac{n_s}{n_p} = \frac{I_p}{I_s}$$

where V_s=secondary voltage
V_p=primary voltage
n_s=number of turns on secondary coil
n_p=number of turns on primary coil
I_p=primary current
I_s=secondary current

Problem: If a step-up transformer has 500 turns on its primary coil and 800 turns on its secondary coil, what will be the output (secondary) voltage be if the primary coil is supplied with 120 V?

Solution:

$$\frac{V_s}{V_p} = \frac{n_s}{n_p}$$

$$V_s = \frac{n_s}{n_p} \times V_p = \frac{800}{500} \times 120V = 192V$$

Skill 7.17 Solve and analyze problems involving alternating currents (e.g., peak current, root mean square current, frequency, reactance, resonant frequency, impedance).

Alternating current (AC) is a type of electrical current with cyclically varying magnitude and direction. This is differentiated from direct current (DC), which has constant direction. AC is the type of current delivered to businesses and residences.

Though other waveforms are sometimes used, the vast majority of AC current is sinusoidal. Thus we can use wave terminology to help us describe AC current. Since AC current is a function of time, we can express it mathematically as:

$$v(t) = V_{peak} \cdot \sin(\omega t)$$

where V_{peak}= the peak voltage; the maximum value of the voltage

ω=angular frequency; a measure of rotation rate

t=time

A few more terms are useful to help us characterize AC current:

Peak-to-peak value: The difference between the positive and negative peak values. Thus peak-to-peak value is equal to 2 x V_{peak}.

Root mean square value (V_{rms}, I_{rms}): A specific type of average found by the following formulae:

$$V_{rms} = \frac{V_{peak}}{\sqrt{2}} \quad ; \quad I_{rms} = \frac{I_{peak}}{\sqrt{2}} ; \quad I_{rms} = \frac{V_{rms}}{R}$$

V_{rms} is useful because an AC current will deliver the same power as a DC current if its V_{rms}=V_{DC}, i.e. average power $P_{av} = V_{rms} I_{rms}$.

Frequency: Describes how often the wave passes through a particular point per unit time. Note that this is physical frequency, f, which is related to the angular frequency ω by:

$$\omega = 2\pi f$$

Resonant frequency: The frequency at which the impedance between the input and output of the circuit is minimum. At this frequency a phenomenon known as electrical resonance occurs.

Impedance: A measure of opposition to an alternating current. It is similar to resistance and also has the unit ohm. However, due to the phased nature of AC, impedance is a complex number, having both real and imaginary components. The resistance is the real part of impedance while the reactance of capacitors and inductors constitute the imaginary part.

Reactance: The impedance contributed by inductors and capacitors in AC circuit. Mathematically, reactance is the imaginary part of impedance. The relationship between impedance (Z), resistance(R), and reactance (X) is given by below.

$$Z = R + Xi$$

1. Remember that $i = \sqrt{-1}$

Problem:

An AC current has V_{rms}=220 V. What is its peak-to-peak value?

Solution:

We simply determine V_{peak} from the definition of V_{rms}:

$$V_{rms} = \frac{V_{peak}}{\sqrt{2}}$$

$$V_{peak} = V_{rms} \times \sqrt{2} = 220V \times \sqrt{2} = 311.12V$$

Therefore,

$$V_{peak-to-peak} = 2 \times V_{peak} = 2 \times 311.12V = 622.24V$$

Skill 7.18 Identify principles and components underlying the operation of motors and generators.

Motors

Electric motors are found in many common appliances such as fans and washing machines. The operation of a motor is based on the principle that a magnetic field exerts a force on a current carrying conductor. This force is essentially due to the fact that the current carrying conductor itself generates a magnetic field; the basic principle that governs the behavior of an electromagnet. In a motor, this idea is used to convert **electrical energy into mechanical energy**, most commonly rotational energy. Thus the components of the simplest motors must include a strong magnet and a current-carrying coil placed in the magnetic field in such a way that the force on it causes it to rotate.

Motors may be run using DC or AC current and may be designed in a number of ways with varying levels of complexity. A very basic DC motor consists of the following components:

- A **field magnet**
- An **armature** with a coil around it that rotates between the poles of the field magnet
- A **power supply** that supplies current to the armature
- An **axle** that transfers the rotational energy of the armature to the working parts of the motor
- A set of **commutators** and **brushes** that reverse the direction of power flow every half rotation so that the armature continues to rotate

Generators

Generators are devices that are the opposite of motors in that they convert **mechanical energy into electrical energy**. The mechanical energy can come from a variety of sources; combustion engines, blowing wind, falling water, or even a hand crank or bicycle wheel.

Most generators rely upon electromagnetic induction to create an electrical current. These generators basically consist of magnets and a coil. The magnets create a magnetic field and the coil is located within this field. Mechanical energy, from whatever source, is used to spin the coil within this field. As stated by Faraday's Law, this produces a voltage. It is important to understand that generators move electric current, but do not create electrical charge. We can make an analogy to a water pump, which can create water current, but does not create water.

Skill 7.19 Calculate and analyze the magnetic fields around current carrying conductors (e.g., long straight wires, loops, solenoids).

Conductors through which electrical currents travel will produce magnetic fields: The magnetic field dB induced at a distance r by an element of current Idl flowing through a wire element of length dl is given by the **Biot-Savart** law

$$dB = \frac{\mu_0}{4\pi} \frac{Idl \times \hat{r}}{r^2}$$

where μ_0 is a constant known as the permeability of free space and $\hat{r}$ is the unit vector pointing from the current element to the point where the magnetic field is calculated.

An alternate statement of this law is Ampere's law according to which the line integral of $B.dl$ around any closed path enclosing a steady current I is given by

$$\oint_C B \cdot dl = \mu_0 I$$

The basis of this phenomenon is the same no matter what the shape of the conductor, but we will consider three common situations:

Straight Wire

Around a current-carrying straight wire, the magnetic field lines form concentric circles around the wire. The direction of the magnetic field is given by the right-hand rule: When the thumb of the right hand points in the direction of the current, the fingers curl around the wire in the direction of the magnetic field. Note the direction of the current and magnetic field in the diagram.

To find the magnetic field of an infinitely long (allowing us to disregarding end effects) we apply Ampere's Law to a circular path at a distance r around the wire:

$$B = \frac{\mu_0 I}{2\pi r}$$

where μ_0=the permeability of free space (4π x 10^{-7} T·m/A)
I=current
r=distance from the wire

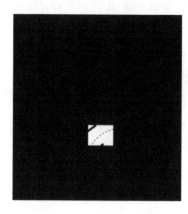

Loops

Like the straight wire from which it's been made, a looped wire has magnetic field lines that form concentric circles with direction following the right-hand rule. However, the field are additive in the center of the loop creating a field like the one shown. The magnetic field of a loop is found similarly to that for a straight wire.

In the center of the loop, the magnetic field is:

$$B = \frac{\mu_0 I}{2r}$$

Solenoids

A solenoid is essentially a coil of conduction wire wrapped around a central object. This means it is a series of loops and the magnetic field is similarly a sum of the fields that would form around several loops, as shown.

The magnetic field of a solenoid can be found as with the following equation:

$$B = \mu_0 n I$$

In this equation, n is turn density, which is simply the number of turns divided by the length of the solenoid.

COMPETENCY VIII.   KNOWLEDGE OF MODERN PHYSICS

Skill 8.1   Solve and analyze problems based upon the energy of a photon (e.g., photoelectric effect, E=hf).

The wave theory of light explains many different phenomena but falls short when describing effects such as **blackbody radiation** and the **photoelectric effect**. In trying to derive the spectral distribution of blackbody radiation, Max Planck proposed that an atom can absorb or emit energy only in chunks known as quanta. The energy E contained in each quantum depends on the frequency of the radiation and is given by $E = hf$ where Planck's constant $h = 6.626 \times 10^{-34}\, J.s = 4.136 \times 10^{-15}\, eV.s$.

Einstein extended this idea further to suggest that quantization is a fundamental property of electromagnetic radiation which consists of quanta of energy known as **photons**. The energy of each photon is hf where h is Planck's constant.

Problem: A light beam has an intensity of 2W and wavelength of 600nm. What is the energy of each photon in the beam? How many photons are emitted by the beam every second?

Solution: The energy of each photon is given by
$E = hc/\lambda = 6.626 \times 10^{-34} \times 3 \times 10^{8} / (600 \times 10^{-9}) = 3.31 \times 10^{-19}\, J$.
The number of photons emitted each second = $2/(3.31 \times 10^{-19}) = 6.04 \times 10^{18}$.

Einstein used the photon hypothesis to explain the photoelectric effect which is the emission of electrons from a metal surface when light is incident on it. When this metal surface is a cathode with the anode held at a higher potential V, an electric current flows in the external circuit. It is observed that current flows only for light of higher frequencies. Also there is a threshold negative potential, the **stopping potential** V_0 below which no current will flow in the circuit.

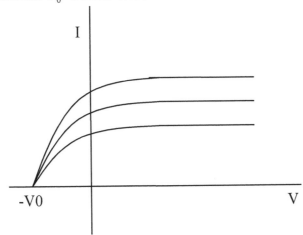

The figure displayed above shows current flow vs. potential for three different intensities of light. It shows that the maximum current flow increases with increasing light intensity but the stopping potential remains the same.

All these observations are counter-intuitive if one considers light to be a wave but may be understood in terms of light particles or photons. According to this interpretation, each photon transfers its energy to a single electron in the metal. Since the energy of a photon depends on its frequency, only a photon of higher frequency can transfer enough energy to an electron to enable it to pass the stopping potential threshold.

When V is negative, only electrons with a kinetic energy greater than $|eV|$ can reach the anode. The maximum kinetic energy of the emitted electrons is given by eV_0. This is expressed by Einstein's photoelectric equation as

$$(\tfrac{1}{2}mv^2)_{max} = eV_0 = hf - \varphi$$

where the **work function** φ is the energy needed to release an electron from the metal and is characteristic of the metal.

Problem: The work function for potassium is 2.20eV. What is the stopping potential for light of wavelength 400nm?

Solution:
$eV_0 = hf - \varphi = hc/\lambda - \varphi = 4.136 \times 10^{-15} \times 3 \times 10^8 / (400 \times 10^{-9}) - 2.20 = 3.10 - 2.20 = 0.90\text{eV}$
    Thus stopping potential $V_0 = 0.90\text{V}$

The particle nature of light also explains the **Compton effect** in which x-rays are scattered by free electrons. The lower frequency of the scattered x-rays may be calculated from a model that treats the scattering as a collision between two particles, an electron and a photon.

Skill 8.2 Identify Einstein's postulates of special relativity and analyze their implications (e.g., Lorentz contraction, time dilation).

Albert Einstein proposed his *special theory of relativity* in 1905. This formed part of his research article, "On the Electrodynamics of Moving Bodies". Nearly three centuries earlier, Galileo stated that all uniform motion was relative and there was no absolute, well-defined state of rest. For example, a person sitting in his deck chair on a ship may seem to be resting but someone watching him from far will notice movement. Einstein's theory combines Galilean relativity with the idea that all observers will always measure the speed of light to be the same regardless of their linear motion.

This theory has a variety of surprising consequences that seem to violate common sense but were verified experimentally. This theory was called special because it applies the principle of relativity only to inertial frames. Another important thing is that special relativity reveals that c is not just the velocity of a certain phenomenon, light, but rather a fundamental feature of the way space and time are tied together. In particular, special relativity states that it is impossible for any material object to accelerate to light speed.

Postulates: The two postulates of special relativity are
1. Special principle of relativity: The laws of physics are same in all inertial frames of reference which simply means that there are no privileged inertial frames of reference.

2. Invariance of c: The speed of light in a vacuum is a universal constant (c) which is independent of the motion of the light source.

Now let us look at two important consequences of special relativity.
1. Lorentz contraction: Relativity theory depends on "reference frames". An inertial reference frame is a point in space at rest or in uniform motion from which a position can be measured along 3 spatial axes. Lorentz contraction can be described as the perceived reduction of the length of an object measured by an observer moving with reference to the object in the direction of its length. This effect is negligible at the speeds we experience everyday but would be noticeable at velocities comparable to that of light.

2. Time dilation: The time lapse between two events is not invariant from one observer to another but is dependent on the relative speeds of the observers' reference frames. Time dilation can also be defined as the difference of time between two ticks in a moving frame and rest frame of the clock. The difference between two ticks measured from a moving frame is larger than the difference between two ticks in the rest frame of a clock.

Skill 8.3   Calculate and analyze applications of Einstein's mass-energy equivalence.

Mass-energy equivalence is the principle that mass is a form of energy. Even when a body of mass m is at rest and has no kinetic energy, it has a **rest energy** E given by Einstein's famous equation $E = mc^2$, a result derived from his special theory of relativity. The total relativistic energy of a body of mass m moving at a velocity v is given by $E = \dfrac{mc^2}{\sqrt{1 - v^2/c^2}}$. We can see that when the body is at rest $v=0$ and rest energy $E = mc^2$.

One consequence of mass-energy equivalence is that the principles of conservation of mass and conservation of energy are combined into the **conservation of mass and energy** as a whole. The other corollary is that mass may be transformed into other types of energy and vice versa.

A notable feature of the transformation of mass into energy is the fact that the conversion factor c^2 is extremely large. Thus a very small mass may yield a stupendous amount of energy, a significant factor in the development of the atomic bomb.

<u>Problem</u>: What is the quantity of energy contained in a 1g mass?

<u>Solution</u>: $E = mc^2 \approx 10^{-3} \times (3 \times 10^8)^2 = 9 \times 10^{13} J$

Another example of the conversion of mass into energy is the **binding energy** of an atomic nucleus. A deuteron, for instance, has a mass that is less than the sum of the masses its constituent parts, a neutron and a proton. The mass difference is the binding energy that holds the deuteron together.

<u>Problem</u>: The mass of a proton is $1.6726 \times 10^{-27} Kg$, the mass of a neutron is $1.6749 \times 10^{-27} Kg$, and the mass of a deuteron is $3.3436 \times 10^{-27} Kg$. What is the binding energy of a deuteron?

<u>Solution</u>: The difference in mass between the deuteron and its constituents $\Delta m =$

$1.6726 \times 10^{-27} + 1.6749 \times 10^{-27} - 3.3436 \times 10^{-27} = 0.0039 \times 10^{-27} Kg$

Thus binding energy = $\Delta mc^2 = 3.51 \times 10^{-13} J$

Skill 8.4 Calculate and analyze the energy change of an atom when an electron makes an energy-level transition.

The Bohr model of the atom was the first to suggest that electrons orbit a central nucleus in quantified orbits, or energy levels. Electrons exist in certain orbitals around the nucleus when they are in the ground or stable state. However, it is possible for electrons to move between the orbitals or energy levels. In these cases the atom may absorb or emit energy in the form of a photon. The larger the orbit is the higher the energy is. So for an electron to move to a higher orbit or energy level, the atom must be excited by the input of some energy. When an electron drops to a lower orbit, energy is released from the atom and a photon is emitted.

Problem: When a helium electron makes an energy change from the n=4 orbital to the n=3 orbital, a helium atom will emit a photon of wavelength 470 nanometers. Calculate the n=4 energy of the atom, given that the n=3 energy is -6.04 electron volts.

Solution: First we must determine the energy of the photon of light emitted using the equation :

$$E = hc/\lambda$$
$$E = (6.63 \times 10^{-34} \text{ J s}) (3 \times 10^{8} \text{ m/s}) / (470 \times 10^{-9} \text{ m}) = 4.23 \times 10^{-19} \text{ J}$$

We then convert the energy from Joules into electron volts by dividing by 1.6×10^{-19} and so we have that the energy emitted in the photon is 2.63 eV. Since the change in energy is given by the following equation

$$\Delta E = E_f - E_i$$

and we know that E_f is -6.04 eV and ΔE is -2.63eV, it is a simple matter to solve for E_i which turns out to be -3.41 eV. This makes logical sense too because the higher orbit should have the higher, or less negative, energy.

Skill 8.5   Distinguish between the characteristics of alpha, beta, and gamma radiation.

In alpha decay, an atom emits an alpha particle. An alpha particle contains two protons and two neutrons. This makes it identical to a helium nucleus and so an alpha particle may be written as He^{2+} or it can be denoted using the Greek letter α. Because a nucleus decaying through alpha radiation loses protons and neutrons, the mass of the atom loses about 4 Daltons and it actually becomes a different element (transmutation). For instance:

$$^{238}U \rightarrow {}^{234}Th + \alpha$$

Radioactive heavy nuclei including uranium and radium typically decay by emitting alpha particles. The alpha decay often leaves the nucleus in an excited state with the extra energy subsequently removed by gamma radiation. The energy of alpha particles can be readily absorbed by skin or air and so alpha decaying substances are only harmful to living things if they are introduced internally.

Like alpha decay, beta decay involves emission of a particle. In this case, though, it is a beta particle, which is either an electron or positron. Note that a positron is the antimatter equivalent of an electron and so these particles are often denoted β^- and β^+. Beta plus and minus decay occur via roughly opposite paths. In beta minus decay, a neutron is converted in a proton (specifically, a down quark is converted to an up quark), an electron and an anti-neutrino; the latter two are emitted. In beta plus decay, on the other hand, a proton is converted to a neutron, a positron, and a neutrino; again, the latter two are emitted. As in alpha decay, a nucleus undergoing beta decay is transmuted into a different element because the number of protons is altered. However, because the total number of nucleons remains unchanged, the atomic mass remains the same (note, that the neutron is actually slightly heavier than a proton so mass is gained during beta plus decay). So examples of beta decay would be:

$$^{137}_{55}Cs \rightarrow {}^{137}_{56}Ba + e^- + \bar{v}_e \qquad \text{(beta minus decay)}$$

$$^{22}_{11}Na \rightarrow {}^{22}_{10}Ne + e^+ + v_e \qquad \text{(beta plus decay)}$$

Beta decaying isotopes, such as Strontium 90, are commonly used in cancer treatment. These particles are better able to penetrate skin than alpha particles and so exposure to larger amounts of beta particles poses a risk to all living things.

Gamma radiation is quite different from alpha and beta decay in that it does not involve the emission of nucleon-containing particles or the transmutation of elements. Rather, gamma-ray photons are emitted during gamma decay. These gamma rays are a specific form of electromagnetic radiation that results from certain sub-atomic particle contacts. For instance, electron-positron annihilation leads to the emission of gamma rays. More commonly, though, gamma rays are emitted by nuclei left in an excited state following alpha or beta decay. Thus, gamma decay lowers the energy level of a nucleus, but does not change its atomic mass or charge. The high energy content of gamma rays, coupled with their ability to penetrate dense materials, make them a serious risk to living things.

Skill 8.6 Analyze outcomes of radiation processes (e.g., conservation of charge, conservation of mass, balancing of nuclear equation).

In both alpha and beta radiation, the mass and charge of a decaying nucleus are altered. Both charge and mass, however, must always be conserved over all when a nucleus decays. Using the examples given above, we can take a closer look at how this is so in alpha and beta decay.

$$^{238}U \rightarrow {}^{234}Th + \alpha$$

This isotope of uranium weighs 238 Daltons. Because it is uranium, it has 92 protons, meaning it must have 146 neutrons. When it undergoes alpha decay it loses 2 protons and 2 neutrons. The alpha particle weighs 4 Daltons and the nucleus that has undergone decay weighs 234 Daltons. Thus mass is conserved. The decayed nucleus will have a charge reduced by that of 2 protons following the decay. However, the emitted alpha particle carries the additional charge due to its 2 protons. Thus both charge and mass are conserved over all.

$$^{137}_{55}Cs \rightarrow {}^{137}_{56}Ba + e^- + \bar{v}_e$$

This isotope of caesium weighs 137 Daltons and, like all caesium isotopes, it has 55 protons. When it undergoes beta minus decay, a neutron is converted to a proton and an electron and an anti-neutrino are lost. The total mass-energy of the system is conserved since the difference in mass between a neutron and an electron plus proton is balanced by the energy of the emitted electron and the anti-neutrino. In beta minus decay a neutron, with no charge, is split into a positively charged proton and a negatively charged electron. Thus the conservation of charge is satisfied. The electron is emitted, while the proton remains in the nucleus. With one extra proton, the nucleus is now a barium isotope.

$$^{22}_{11}Na \rightarrow {}^{22}_{10}Ne + e^+ + v_e$$

In order to conserve mass-energy of the system, beta plus decay cannot occur in isolation but only in a nucleus since the mass of a neutron is greater than the mass of a proton plus electron. The difference in binding energy of the mother and daughter nucleus provides the additional energy needed for the reaction to go through. Charge is conserved when a positively charged proton is converted into a positively charged positron. With one fewer proton, the decayed nucleus is now a neon isotope weighing 22 Daltons.

Problems involving balancing nuclear equations can involve simple radioactive decay, fission, fusion, and other nuclear processes. In all cases, both mass-energy and charge must be balanced.

Problem: Uranium 235 is used as a nuclear fuel in a chain reaction. The reaction is initiated by a single neutron and produces barium 141, an unknown isotope, and 3 neutrons that can go on to propagate the chain reaction. Determine the unknown isotope. Assume that the kinetic energies and the energy released in the reaction is negligible compared to the masses of the isotopes produced.

Solution: We can begin by writing out the reaction, leaving open the unknown isotope X.

$$^{235}_{92}U + ^{1}_{0}n \rightarrow ^{141}_{56}Ba + X + 3^{1}_{0}n$$

We begin with the charge balance; since the neutron has no charge, the unknown isotope must have 36 protons. Consulting a periodic table, we see that this will mean it is a Krypton isotope. Now we can balance the mass. Since the original nucleus weighed 235 Daltons and one neutron was added to it, the total mass of the resultant nuclei must be 236. So, we can simple subtract the weight of the barium isotope and the 3 new neutrons to find the unknown weight:

$$236-141-3=92$$

Thus our unknown isotope is krypton 92, making the balanced equation:

$$^{235}_{92}U + ^{1}_{0}n \rightarrow ^{141}_{56}Ba + ^{92}_{36}Kr + 3^{1}_{0}n$$

Skill 8.7 Calculate the age of a radioactive source, given data (e.g., half-life, activity, remaining mass, decayed fraction).

While the radioactive decay of an individual atom is impossible to predict, a mass of radioactive material will decay at a specific rate. Radioactive isotopes exhibit exponential decay and we can express this decay in a useful equation as follows:

$$A = A_0 e^{kt}$$

Where A is the amount of radioactive material remaining after time t, A_0 is the original amount of radioactive material, t is the elapsed time, and k is the unique activity of the radioactive material. Note that k is unique to each radioactive isotope and it specifies how quickly the material decays. Sometimes it is convenient to express the rate of decay as half-life. A half-life is the time needed for half a given mass of radioactive material to decay. Thus, after one half-life, 50% of an original mass will have decayed, after two half lives, 75% will have decayed and so on.

Let's examine a sample problem related to radioactive decay.

Problem: Radiocarbon dating has been used extensively to determine the age of fossilized organic remains. It is based on the fact that while most of the carbon atoms in living things is ^{12}C, a small percentage is ^{14}C. Since ^{14}C is a radioactive isotope, it is lost from a fossilized specimen at a specific rate following the death of an organism. The original and current mass of ^{14}C can be inferred from the relative amount of ^{12}C. So, if the half-life of ^{14}C is 5730 years and a specimen that originally contained 1.28 mg of ^{14}C now contains 0.10 mg, how old is the specimen?

In certain problems, we may be simply provided with the activity, k, but in this problem we must use the information given about half-life to solve for k.

Since we know that after one half-life, 50% of the material remains radioactive, we can plug into the governing equation above:

$$A = A_0 e^{kt}$$

$$0.5\,A_0 = A_0 e^{5730k}$$

$$k = (\ln(0.5))/5730 = -0.0001209$$

Having determined k, we can use this same equation again to determine how old the specimen described above must be:

$$A = A_0 e^{kt}$$

$$0.10 = 1.28 e^{-0.0001209t}$$

$$t = \frac{\ln\left(\dfrac{0.10}{1.28}\right)}{-0.0001209} = 21087$$

Thus, the specimen is 21,087 years old.

Note that this same equation can be used to calculate the half-life of an isotope if information regarding the decay after a given number of years were provided.

Skill 8.8 Identify and differentiate between fission and fusion processes and applications.

Nuclear fusion involves the joining of several nuclei to form one heavier nucleus. Nuclear fission is the reverse of fusion, in that it is the splitting of a nucleus to form multiple lighter nuclei. Depending on the weight of the nuclei involved, both fission and fusion may result in either the absorption or release of energy. Iron and nickel have the largest binding energies per nucleon and so are the most stable nuclei. Thus, *fusion* releases energy when the two nuclei are lighter than iron or nickel and *fission* releases energy when the two nuclei are heavier than iron or nickel. Conversely, fusion will absorb energy when the nuclei are heavier and fission will absorb energy when the nuclei are lighter.

Nuclear fusion is common in nature and is the mechanism by which new natural elements are created. Fusion reactions power the stars and (energy absorbing) fusion of heavy elements occurs in supernova explosions. Despite the fact that significant energy is required to trigger the fusion of two nuclei (to overcome the electrostatic repulsion between the positively charged protons), the reaction can be self-sustaining because the energy released by the fusion of two light nuclei is greater than that required to force them together. Fusion is typically much harder to control that fission and so it is not used for power generation though fusion reactions are used to drive hydrogen bombs.

Nuclear fission is unique in that it can be harnessed for a variety of applications. This is done via the use of a chain reaction initiated by the bombardment of certain isotopes with free neutrons. When a nucleus is struck by a free neutron, it splits into smaller nuclei and also produces free neutrons, gamma rays, and alpha and beta particles. The free neutrons can then go onto interact with other nuclei and perpetuate the fission reaction. Isotopes, such as ^{235}U and ^{239}P that sustain the chain reaction are known as fissile and used for nuclear fuel.

Because fission can be controlled via chain reaction, it is used in nuclear power generation. Uncontrolled fission reactions are also used in nuclear weapons, including the atomic bombs developed during the Manhattan Project and exploded over Hiroshima and Nagasaki in 1945.

Though it is currently in use in many locations, nuclear fission for power generation remains somewhat controversial. The amount of available energy per pound in nuclear fuel is millions of times that in fossil fuels. Additionally, nuclear power generation does not produce the air and water pollutants that are problematic byproducts of fossil fuel combustion. The currently used fission reactions, however, do produce radioactive waste that must be contained for thousands of years.

Skill 8.9   Solve and analyze problems involving Heisenberg's uncertainty principle (e.g., momentum vs. position, energy, time).

Heisenberg's uncertainty principle places a limit on the accuracy with which one can measure the properties of a physical system. This limit is not due to the imperfections of measuring instruments or experimental methods but arises from the fundamental wave-particle duality inherent in quantum systems.

One statement of the uncertainty principle is made in terms of the position and momentum of a particle. If Δx is the uncertainty in the position of a particle in one dimension and Δp the uncertainty in its momentum in that dimension, then according to the uncertainty principle

$$\Delta x \Delta p \geq \hbar / 2$$

where the reduced Planck's constant $\hbar = h / 2\pi = 1.05457168 \times 10^{-34} J.s$

Thus if we measure the position of a particle with greater and greater accuracy, at some point the accuracy in the measurement of its momentum will begin to fall. A simple way to understand this is by considering the wave nature of a subatomic particle. If the wave has a single wavelength, then the momentum of the particle is also exactly known using the DeBroglie momentum-wavelength relationship. The position of the wave, however, extends through all space. If waves of several different wavelengths are superposed, the position of the wave becomes increasingly localized as more wavelengths are added. The increased spread in wavelength, however, then results in an increased momentum spread.

An alternate statement of the uncertainty principle may be made in terms of energy and time.

$$\Delta E \Delta t \geq \hbar / 2$$

Thus, for a particle that has a very short lifetime, the uncertainty in the determination of its energy will be large.

<u>Problem</u>: If a proton is confined to a nucleus that is approximately $10^{-15}m$ in diameter, estimate the minimum uncertainty in its momentum in any one dimension.

<u>Solution</u>: The uncertainty of the position of the proton in any dimension cannot be greater than $10^{-15}m$. Using the uncertainty principle we find that the approximate uncertainty in its momentum in any one dimension must be greater than

$\Delta p = \hbar / (2\Delta x) \approx 10^{-19} Kg.m/s$

Skill 8.10 Differentiate between the four quantum number in atoms and their physical significance.

Quantum numbers are useful for describing the quantum states of individual electrons within an atom. Each electron in an atom has a unique set of these four numbers. A value for each of the following numbers must be known to fully describe the state of a given electron.

Principal quantum number: This number denotes the energy level of an electron in an atom. It is typically represented with an *n* and can have values of 1, 2, 3... with higher values representing greater distance from the nucleus. These values also correspond to the "electron shells".

Azimuthal quantum number: This number is also referred to as the angular quantum number or the orbital quantum number and denotes the angular momentum of the orbital. The azimuthal quantum number is represented as *l* and can have integer values from zero to *n-1*. This number specifies the "shape" of an atomic orbital. These orbitals are typically described with letters such that *l*=0 is the s orbital, *l*=1 is the p orbital, *l*=2 is the d orbital and so on. Note that, for a given principal quantum number, there will be *n-1* azimuthal quantum numbers (i.e., an electron with *n*=1 can only have *l*=0 or *l*=1).

Magnetic quantum number: This number specifies the energy shift of an electron due to an external magnetic field and is represented m_l. The magnetic quantum number has integer values between *–l* and *l* (i.e., an electron with l=2 can have m_l= -2,-1, 0,1,2) which indicates how many available energy levels there are within a single atomic subshell.

Spin quantum number: This number indicates the spin of an electron and is denoted m_s. Spin is an intrinsic quantum property of electrons that can be observed on spectral lines. The spin quantum number can only have a value of –½ or ½.

Skill 8.11 Compare models of the atom (e.g., cloud, plum pudding, Bohr, electron).

In the West, the Greek philosophers Democritus and Leucippus first suggested the concept of the atom. They believed that all atoms were made of the same material but that varied sizes and shapes of atoms resulted in the varied properties of different materials. By the 19th century, John Dalton had advanced a theory stating that each element possesses atoms of a unique type. These atoms were also thought to be the smallest pieces of matter which could not be split or destroyed.

Atomic structure began to be better understood when, in 1897, JJ Thompson discovered the electron while working with cathode ray tubes. Thompson realized the negatively charged electrons were subatomic particles and formulated the "plum pudding model" of the atom to explain how the atom could still have a neutral charge overall. In this model, the negatively charged electrons were randomly present and free to move within a soup or cloud of positive charge. Thompson likened this to the dried fruit that is distributed within the English dessert plum pudding though the electrons were free to move in his model. Ernest Rutherford disproved this model with the discovery of the nucleus in 1909. Rutherford proposed a new "planetary" model of the atom in which electrons orbited around a positively charged nucleus like planets around the sun. Over the next 20 years, protons and neutrons (subnuclear particles) were discovered while additional experiments showed the inadequacy of the planetary model.

As quantum theory was developed and popularized (primarily by Max Planck and Albert Einstein), chemists and physicists began to consider how it might apply to atomic structure. Niels Bohr put forward a model of the atom in which electrons could only orbit the nucleus in circular orbitals with specific distances from the nucleus, energy levels, and angular momentums. In this model, electrons could only make instantaneous "quantum leaps" between the fixed energy levels of the various orbitals. The Bohr model of the atom was altered slightly by Arnold Sommerfeld in 1916 to reflect the fact that the orbitals were elliptical instead of round.

Though the Bohr model is still thought to be largely correct, it was discovered that electrons do not truly occupy neat, cleanly defined orbitals. Rather, they exist as more of an "electron cloud." The work of Louis de Broglie, Erwin Schrödinger, and Werner Heisenberg showed that an electron can actually be located at any distance from the nucleus. However, we can find the *probability* that the electrons exists at given energy levels (i.e., in particular orbitals) and those probabilities will show that the electrons are most frequently organized within the orbitals originally described in the Bohr model.

Skill 8.12 Compare characteristics of subatomic particles (i.e., photons, electrons, neutrinos, neutrons, protons, quarks, antiparticles).

There are two types of elementary particles: **fermions** and **bosons**. Bosons have integer spin, while fermions have half integer spin.

While there are many subatomic bosons, the most familiar one is the **photon**. A photon has zero mass and charge; in a vacuum, a photon travels at the speed of light. Photons do not spontaneously decay, but can be emitted or absorbed by atoms via a number of natural processes. In fact, photons compose all forms of light and mediate electromagnetic interactions.

The two types of fermions are quarks and leptons.

Quarks: Quarks are found nearly exclusively as components of neutrons and protons. They come in three types of arbitrarily named flavors: up, charm, and top (which have a charge of +2/3) and down, strange, and bottom (which have a charge of −1/3. The flavors have varying mass which must be found via indirect methods.

Leptons: Unlike quarks, leptons do not experience strong nuclear force. There are three flavors of leptons; the muon, the tau, and the electron. Each type of lepton consists of a massive charged particle with the same name as the flavor and a smaller neutral particle. This nearly massless neutral particle is called a **neutrino**. Each lepton has a charge of +1 or −1.

Quarks and leptons combine to form the subatomic particles listed below. In each case, we can compare charge, make-up, mass, location, and mobility of the particle.

Electrons: Electrons are a specific type of lepton that exist outside of the nucleus in positions that are functions of their energy levels. Their arrangement and interactions are key to all chemical bonding and reactions. During such chemical processes, electrons can easily be transferred from one atom to another. The charge of an electron is defined as −1 in atomic units (actual charge is -1.6022×10^{-19} coulomb) and the mass of an electron is $^{1}/_{1836}$ of that of a proton.

Protons: Protons are confined inside the atomic nucleus and have a defined charge of +1 atomic units (1.602×10^{-19} coulomb). The mass of a proton is 1 Dalton (or 1 atomic mass unit). Protons may be lost from the nucleus in certain types of radioactive decay. A proton is composed of 2 up quarks and one down quark.

Neutrons: Like protons, neutrons are confined to the nucleus and only lost during certain types of radioactive decay. Neutrons are uncharged particles with assigned mass of 1 Da (in reality neutrons are slightly heavier than protons). A neutron is composed of 2 down quarks and one up quark.

Finally, for each type of subatomic particle, there is an associated **antiparticle** which has the same mass and opposite charge. Given appropriate quantum conditions, particle/antiparticle pairs can destroy each other.

Sample Test

DIRECTIONS: Read each item and select the best response.

1. **Which statement best describes a valid approach to testing a scientific hypothesis?**
(Easy)

   A. Use computer simulations to verify the hypothesis

   B. Perform a mathematical analysis of the hypothesis

   C. Design experiments to test the hypothesis

   D. All of the above

2. **Which description best describes the role of a scientific model of a physical phenomenon?**
(Average Rigor)

   A. An explanation that provides a reasonably accurate approximation of the phenomenon

   B. A theoretical explanation that describes exactly what is taking place

   C. A purely mathematical formulation of the phenomenon

   D. A predictive tool that has no interest in what is actually occurring

3. **Which situation calls might best be described as involving an ethical dilemma for a scientist?**
(Rigorous)

   A. Submission to a peer-review journal of a paper that refutes an established theory

   B. Synthesis of a new radioactive isotope of an element

   C. Use of a computer for modeling a newly-constructed nuclear reactor

   D. Use of a pen-and-paper approach to a difficult problem

4. **Which of the following is not a key purpose for the use of open communication about and peer-review of the results of scientific investigations?**
(Average Rigor)

A. Testing, by other scientists, of the results of an investigation for the purpose of refuting any evidence contrary to an established theory

B. Testing, by other scientists, of the results of an investigation for the purpose of finding or eliminating any errors in reasoning or measurement

C. Maintaining an open, public process to better promote honesty and integrity in science

D. Provide a forum to help promote progress through mutual sharing and review of the results of investigations

5. **Which of the following aspects of the use of computers for collecting experimental data is not a concern for the scientist?**
(Rigorous)

A. The relative speeds of the processor, peripheral, memory storage unit and any other components included in data acquisition equipment

B. The financial cost of the equipment, utilities and maintenance

C. Numerical error due to a lack of infinite precision in digital equipment

D. The order of complexity of data analysis algorithms

6. **If a particular experimental observation contradicts a theory, what is the most appropriate approach that a physicist should take?**
(Average Rigor)

A. Immediately reject the theory and begin developing a new theory that better fits the observed results

B. Report the experimental result in the literature without further ado

C. Repeat the observations and check the experimental apparatus for any potential faulty components or human error, and then compare the results once more with the theory

D. Immediately reject the observation as in error due to its conflict with theory

7. **Which of the following is *not* an SI unit?**
(Average Rigor)

A. Joule

B. Coulomb

C. Newton

D. Erg

8. **Which of the following best describes the relationship of precision and accuracy in scientific measurements?**
(Easy)

A. Accuracy is how well a particular measurement agrees with the value of the actual parameter being measured; precision is how well a particular measurement agrees with the average of other measurements taken for the same value

B. Precision is how well a particular measurement agrees with the value of the actual parameter being measured; accuracy is how well a particular measurement agrees with the average of other measurements taken for the same value

C. Accuracy is the same as precision

D. Accuracy is a measure of numerical error; precision is a measure of human error

9. **Which statement best describes a rationale for the use of statistical analysis in characterizing the numerical results of a scientific experiment or investigation?**
    (Average Rigor)

    A. Experimental results need to be adjusted, through the use of statistics, to conform to theoretical predictions and computer models

    B. Since experiments are prone to a number of errors and uncertainties, statistical analysis provides a method for characterizing experimental measurements by accounting for or quantifying these undesirable effects

    C. Experiments are not able to provide any useful information, and statistical analysis is needed to impose a theoretical framework on the results

    D. Statistical analysis is needed to relate experimental measurements to computer-simulated values

10. **Which statement best characterizes the relationship of mathematics and experimentation in physics?**
    (Easy)

    A. Experimentation has no bearing on the mathematical models that are developed for physical phenomena

    B. Mathematics is a tool that assists in the development of models for various physical phenomena as they are studied experimentally, with observations of the phenomena being a test of the validity of the mathematical model

    C. Mathematics is used to test the validity of experimental apparatus for physical measurements

    D. Mathematics is an abstract field with no relationship to concrete experimentation

11. Which of the following mathematical tools would not typically be used for the analysis of an electromagnetic phenomenon?
(Rigorous)

A. Trigonometry

B. Vector calculus

C. Group theory

D. Numerical methods

12. For a problem that involves parameters that vary in rate with direction and location, which of the following mathematical tools would most likely be of greatest value?
(Rigorous)

A. Trigonometry

B. Numerical analysis

C. Group theory

D. Vector calculus

13. Which of the following devices would be best suited for an experiment designed to measure alpha particle emissions from a sample?
(Average Rigor)

A. Photomultiplier tube

B. Thermocouple

C. Geiger-Müller tube

D. Transistor

14. Which of the following experiments presents the most likely cause for concern about laboratory safety?
(Average Rigor)

A. Computer simulation of a nuclear reactor

B. Vibration measurement with a laser

C. Measurement of fluorescent light intensity with a battery-powered photodiode circuit

D. Ambient indoor ionizing radiation measurement with a Geiger counter.

15. A brick and hammer fall from a ledge at the same time. They would be expected to:
(Easy)

   A. Reach the ground at the same time

   B. Accelerate at different rates due to difference in weight

   C. Accelerate at different rates due to difference in potential energy

   D. Accelerate at different rates due to difference in kinetic energy

16. A baseball is thrown with an initial velocity of 30 m/s at an angle of 45°. Neglecting air resistance, how far away will the ball land?
(Rigorous)

   A. 92 m

   B. 78 m

   C. 65 m

   D. 46 m

17. A skateboarder accelerates down a ramp, with constant acceleration of two meters per second squared, from rest. The distance in meters, covered after four seconds, is:
(Rigorous)

   A. 10

   B. 16

   C. 23

   D. 37

18. When acceleration is plotted versus time, the area under the graph represents:
(Average Rigor)

   A. Time

   B. Distance

   C. Velocity

   D. Acceleration

19. An inclined plane is tilted by gradually increasing the angle of elevation θ, until the block will slide down at a constant velocity. The coefficient of friction, μk, is given by:
(Rigorous)

A. cos θ

B. sin θ

C. cosecant θ

D. tangent θ

20. An object traveling through air loses part of its energy of motion due to friction. Which statement best describes what has happened to this energy?
(Easy)

A. The energy is destroyed

B. The energy is converted to static charge

C. The energy is radiated as electromagnetic waves

D. The energy is lost to heating of the air

21. The weight of an object on the earth's surface is designated x. When it is two earth's radii from the surface of the earth, its weight will be:
(Rigorous)

A. x/4

B. x/9

C. 4x

D. 16x

22. Which of the following units is not used to measure torque?
(Average Rigor)

A. slug ft

B. lb ft

C. N m

D. dyne cm

23. A uniform pole weighing 100 grams, that is one meter in length, is supported by a pivot at 40 centimeters from the left end. In order to maintain static position, a 200 gram mass must be placed _____ centimeters from the left end.
(Rigorous)

A. 10

B. 45

C. 35

D. 50

24. The magnitude of a force is:
(Easy)

A. Directly proportional to mass and inversely to acceleration

B. Inversely proportional to mass and directly to acceleration

C. Directly proportional to both mass and acceleration

D. Inversely proportional to both mass and acceleration

25. A projectile with a mass of 1.0 kg has a muzzle velocity of 1500.0 m/s when it is fired from a cannon with a mass of 500.0 kg. If the cannon slides on a frictionless track, it will recoil with a velocity of ____ m/s.
(Rigorous)

A. 2.4

B. 3.0

C. 3.5

D. 1500

26. A car (mass m_1) is driving at velocity v, when it smashes into an unmoving car (mass m_2), locking bumpers. Both cars move together at the same velocity. The common velocity will be given by:
(Rigorous)

A. m_1v/m_2

B. m_2v/m_1

C. $m_1v/(m_1 + m_2)$

D. $(m_1 + m_2)v/m_1$

27. A satellite is in a circular orbit above the earth. Which statement is false?
(Average Rigor)

A. An external force causes the satellite to maintain orbit.

B. The satellite's inertia causes it to maintain orbit.

C. The satellite is accelerating toward the earth.

D. The satellite's velocity and acceleration are not in the same direction.

28. A 100 g mass revolving around a fixed point, on the end of a 0.5 meter string, circles once every 0.25 seconds. What is the magnitude of the centripetal acceleration?
(Average Rigor)

A. 1.23 m/s²

B. 31.6 m/s²

C. 100 m/s²

D. 316 m/s²

29. Which statement best describes the relationship of simple harmonic motion to a simple pendulum of length L, mass m and displacement of arc length s?
(Average Rigor)

A. A simple pendulum cannot be modeled using simple harmonic motion

B. A simple pendulum may be modeled using the same expression as Hooke's law for displacement s, but with a spring constant equal to the tension on the string

C. A simple pendulum may be modeled using the same expression as Hooke's law but with a spring constant equal to m g/L

D. A simple pendulum typically does not undergo simple harmonic motion

30. A mass of 2 kg connected to a spring undergoes simple harmonic motion at a frequency of 3 Hz. What is the spring constant?
(Average Rigor)

A. 6 kg/s²

B. 18 kg/s²

C. 710 kg/s²

D. 1000 kg/s²

31. The kinetic energy of an object is _____ proportional to its _____.
(Average Rigor)

    A. Inversely...inertia

    B. Inversely...velocity

    C. Directly...mass

    D. Directly...time

33. An office building entry ramp uses the principle of which simple machine?
(Easy)

    A. Lever

    B. Pulley

    C. Wedge

    D. Inclined Plane

32. A force is given by the vector 5 N x + 3 N y (where x and y are the unit vectors for the x- and y- axes, respectively). This force is applied to move a 10 kg object 5 m, in the x direction. How much work was done?
(Rigorous)

    A. 250 J

    B. 400 J

    C. 40 J

    D. 25 J

34. If the internal energy of a system remains constant, how much work is done by the system if 1 kJ of heat energy is added?
(Average Rigor)

    A. 0 kJ

    B. -1 kJ

    C. 1 kJ

    D. 3.14 kJ

35. A calorie is the amount of heat energy that will:
(Easy)

   A. Raise the temperature of one gram of water from 14.5º C to 15.5º C.

   B. Lower the temperature of one gram of water from 16.5º C to 15.5º C

   C. Raise the temperature of one gram of water from 32º F to 33º F

   D. Cause water to boil at two atmospheres of pressure.

36. An ice block at 0º Celsius is dropped into 100 g of liquid water at 18º Celsius. When thermal equilibrium is achieved, only liquid water at 0º Celsius is left. What was the mass, in grams, of the original block of ice? Given:
   1. Heat of fusion of ice = 80 cal/g
   2. Heat of vaporization of ice = 540 cal/g
   3. Specific Heat of ice = 0.50 cal/gºC
   4. Specific Heat of water = 1 cal/gºC
   (Rigorous)

   A. 2.0

   B. 5.0

   C. 10.0

   D. 22.5

37. Heat transfer by electromagnetic waves is termed:
(Easy)

   A. Conduction

   B. Convection

   C. Radiation

   D. Phase Change

38. A cooking thermometer in an oven works because the metals it is composed of have different:
(Average Rigor)

   A. Melting points

   B. Heat convection

   C. Magnetic fields

   D. Coefficients of expansion

39. **Which of the following is not an assumption upon which the kinetic-molecular theory of gases is based?**
(Rigorous)

A. Quantum mechanical effects may be neglected

B. The particles of a gas may be treated statistically

C. The particles of the gas are treated as very small masses

D. Collisions between gas particles and container walls are inelastic

40. **What is temperature?**
(Average Rigor)

A. Temperature is a measure of the conductivity of the atoms or molecules in a material

B. Temperature is a measure of the kinetic energy of the atoms or molecules in a material

C. Temperature is a measure of the relativistic mass of the atoms or molecules in a material

D. Temperature is a measure of the angular momentum of electrons in a material

41. **Solids expand when heated because:**
(Rigorous)

A. Molecular motion causes expansion

B. $PV = nRT$

C. Magnetic forces stretch the chemical bonds

D. All material is effectively fluid

42. **What should be the behavior of an electroscope, which has been grounded in the presence of a positively charged object (1), after the ground connection is removed and then the charged object is removed from the vicinity (2)?**
(Average Rigor)

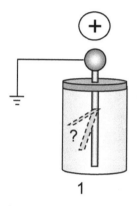

A. The metal leaf will start deflected (1) and then relax to an undeflected position (2)

B. The metal leaf will start in an undeflected position (1) and then be deflected (2)

C. The metal leaf will remain undeflected in both cases

D. The metal leaf will be deflected in both cases

43. **The electric force in Newtons, on two small objects (each charged to − 10 microCoulombs and separated by 2 meters) is:**
(Rigorous)

A. 1.0

B. 9.81

C. 31.0

D. 0.225

44. **A 10 ohm resistor and a 50 ohm resistor are connected in parallel. If the current in the 10 ohm resistor is 5 amperes, the current (in amperes) running through the 50 ohm resistor is:**
(Rigorous)

A. 1

B. 50

C. 25

D. 60

45. How much power is dissipated through the following resistive circuit?
(Average Rigor)

A. 0 W

B. 0.22 W

C. 0.31 W

D. 0.49 W

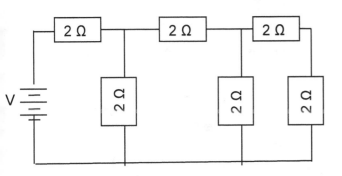

46. The greatest number of 100 watt lamps that can be connected in parallel with a 120 volt system without blowing a 5 amp fuse is:
(Rigorous)

A. 24

B. 12

C. 6

D. 1

47. Which of the following statements may be taken as a legitimate inference based upon the Maxwell equation that states $\nabla \cdot \mathbf{B} = 0$?
(Average Rigor)

A. The electric and magnetic fields are decoupled

B. The electric and magnetic fields are mediated by the W boson

C. There are no photons

D. There are no magnetic monopoles

48. What effect might an applied external magnetic field have on the magnetic domains of a ferromagnetic material?
(Rigorous)

A. The domains that are not aligned with the external field increase in size, but those that are aligned decrease in size

B. The domains that are not aligned with the external field decrease in size, but those that are aligned increase in size

C. The domains align perpendicular to the external field

D. There is no effect on the magnetic domains

49. **What is the effect of running current in the same direction along two parallel wires, as shown below?**
(Rigorous)

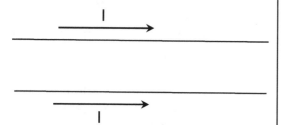

A. There is no effect

B. The wires attract one another

C. The wires repel one another

D. A torque is applied to both wires

50. **The current induced in a coil is defined by which of the following laws?**
(Easy)

A. Lenz's Law

B. Burke's Law

C. The Law of Spontaneous Combustion

D. Snell's Law

51. **A light bulb is connected in series with a rotating coil within a magnetic field. The brightness of the light may be increased by any of the following except:**
(Average Rigor)

A. Rotating the coil more rapidly.

B. Using more loops in the coil.

C. Using a different color wire for the coil.

D. Using a stronger magnetic field.

52. **What is the direction of the magnetic field at the center of the loop of current (I) shown below (i.e., at point A)?**
(Easy)

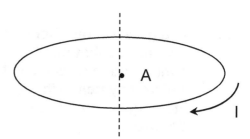

A. Down, along the axis (dotted line)
B. Up, along the axis (dotted line)
C. The magnetic field is oriented in a radial direction
D. There is no magnetic field at point A

53. The use of two circuits next to each other, with a change in current in the primary circuit, demonstrates:
(Rigorous)

A. Mutual current induction

B. Dielectric constancy

C. Harmonic resonance

D. Resistance variation

54. A semi-conductor allows current to flow:
(Easy)

A. Never

B. Always

C. As long as it stays below a maximum temperature

D. When a minimum voltage is applied

55. All of the following use semi-conductor technology, except a(n):
(Average Rigor)

A. Transistor

B. Diode

C. Capacitor

D. Operational Amplifier

56. A wave generator is used to create a succession of waves. The rate of wave generation is one every 0.33 seconds. The period of these waves is:
(Average Rigor)

A. 2.0 seconds

B. 1.0 seconds

C. 0.33 seconds

D. 3.0 seconds

57. An electromagnetic wave propagates through a vacuum. Independent of its wavelength, it will move with constant:
(Easy)

   A. Acceleration

   B. Velocity

   C. Induction

   D. Sound

58. A wave has speed 60 m/s and wavelength 30,000 m. What is the frequency of the wave?
(Average Rigor)

   A. 2.0×10^{-3} Hz

   B. 60 Hz

   C. 5.0×10^2 Hz

   D. 1.8×10^6 Hz

59. Rainbows are created by:
(Easy)

   A. Reflection, dispersion, and recombination

   B. Reflection, resistance, and expansion

   C. Reflection, compression, and specific heat

   D. Reflection, refraction, and dispersion

60. Which of the following is *not* a legitimate explanation for refraction of light rays at boundaries between different media?
(Rigorous)

   A. Light seeks the path of least time between two different points

   B. Due to phase matching and other boundary conditions, plane waves travel in different directions on either side of the boundary, depending on the material parameters

   C. The electric and magnetic fields become decoupled at the boundary

   D. Light rays obey Snell's law

61. A stationary sound source produces a wave of frequency *F*. An observer at position A is moving toward the horn, while an observer at position B is moving away from the horn. Which of the following is true?
(Rigorous)

A. $F_A < F < F_B$

B. $F_B < F < F_A$

C. $F < F_A < F_B$

D. $F_B < F_A < F$

62. A monochromatic ray of light passes from air to a thick slab of glass (n = 1.41) at an angle of 45° from the normal. At what angle does it leave the air/glass interface?
(Rigorous)

A. 45°

B. 30°

C. 15°

D. 55°

63. If one sound is ten decibels louder than another, the ratio of the intensity of the first to the second is:
(Average Rigor)

A. 20:1

B. 10:1

C. 1:1

D. 1:10

64. The velocity of sound is greatest in:
(Average Rigor)

A. Water

B. Steel

C. Alcohol

D. Air

65. **A vibrating string's frequency is _____ proportional to the _____.**
(Rigorous)

A. Directly; Square root of the tension

B. Inversely; Length of the string

C. Inversely; Squared length of the string

D. Inversely; Force of the plectrum

66. **Which of the following apparatus can be used to measure the wavelength of a sound produced by a tuning fork?**
(Average Rigor)

A. A glass cylinder, some water, and iron filings

B. A glass cylinder, a meter stick, and some water

C. A metronome and some ice water

D. A comb and some tissue

67. **The highest energy is associated with:**
(Easy)

A. UV radiation

B. Yellow light

C. Infrared radiation

D. Gamma radiation

68. **An object two meters tall is speeding toward a plane mirror at 10 m/s. What happens to the image as it nears the surface of the mirror?**
(Rigorous)

A. It becomes inverted.

B. The Doppler Effect must be considered.

C. It remains two meters tall.

D. It changes from a real image to a virtual image.

69. **Automobile mirrors that have a sign, "objects are closer than they appear" say so because:**
(Rigorous)

A. The real image of an obstacle, through a converging lens, appears farther away than the object.

B. The real or virtual image of an obstacle, through a converging mirror, appears farther away than the object.

C. The real image of an obstacle, through a diverging lens, appears farther away than the object.

D. The virtual image of an obstacle, through a diverging mirror, appears farther away than the object.

70. **If an object is 20 cm from a convex lens whose focal length is 10 cm, the image is:**
(Rigorous)

A. Virtual and upright

B. Real and inverted

C. Larger than the object

D. Smaller than the object

71. **The constant of proportionality between the energy and the frequency of electromagnetic radiation is known as the:**
(Easy)

A. Rydberg constant

B. Energy constant

C. Planck constant

D. Einstein constant

72. **Which phenomenon was first explained using the concept of quantization of energy, thus providing one of the key foundational principles for the later development of quantum theory?**
(Rigorous)

A. The photoelectric effect

B. Time dilation

C. Blackbody radiation

D. Magnetism

73. **Which statement best describes why population inversion is necessary for a laser to operate?**
(Rigorous)

   A. Population inversion prevents too many electrons from being excited into higher energy levels, thus preventing damage to the gain medium.

   B. Population inversion maintains a sufficient number of electrons in a higher energy state so as to allow a significant amount of stimulated emission.

   C. Population inversion prevents the laser from producing coherent light.

   D. Population inversion is not necessary for the operation of most lasers.

74. **Bohr's theory of the atom was the first to quantize:**
(Average Rigor)

   A. Work

   B. Angular Momentum

   C. Torque

   D. Duality

75. **Two neutral isotopes of a chemical element have the same numbers of:**
(Easy)

   A. Electrons and Neutrons

   B. Electrons and Protons

   C. Protons and Neutrons

   D. Electrons, Neutrons, and Protons

76. **When a radioactive material emits an alpha particle only, its atomic number will:**
(Average Rigor)

   A. Decrease

   B. Increase

   C. Remain unchanged

   D. Change randomly

77. **Ten grams of a sample of a radioactive material (half-life = 12 days) were stored for 48 days and re-weighed. The new mass of material was:**
(Rigorous)

   A. 1.25 g

   B. 2.5 g

   C. 0.83 g

   D. 0.625 g

78. **Which of the following pairs of elements are not found to fuse in the centers of stars?**
    (Average Rigor)

    A. Oxygen and Helium

    B. Carbon and Hydrogen

    C. Beryllium and Helium

    D. Cobalt and Hydrogen

79. **In a fission reactor, heavy water:**
    (Average Rigor)

    A. Cools off neutrons to control temperature

    B. Moderates fission reactions

    C. Initiates the reaction chain

    D. Dissolves control rods

80. **Given the following values for the masses of a proton, a neutron and an alpha particle, what is the nuclear binding energy of an alpha particle?**
    (Rigorous)

    Proton mass=1.6726 x 10^{-27} kg
    Neutron mass=1.6749 x 10^{-27} kg
    Alpha particle mass= 6.6465 x 10^{-27} kg

    A. 0 J

    B. 7.3417 x 10^{-27} J

    C. 4 J

    D. 4.3589 x 10^{-12} J

Answer Key

1.	D			50.	A	74.	B
2.	A	26.	C	51.	C	75.	B
3.	B	27.	B	52.	A	76.	A
4.	A	28.	D	53.	A	77.	D
5.	D	29.	C	54.	D	78.	D
6.	C	30.	C	55.	C	79.	B
7.	D	31.	C	56.	C	80.	D
8.	A	32.	D	57.	B		
9.	B	33.	D	58.	A		
10.	B	34.	C	59.	D		
11.	C	35.	A	60.	C		
12.	D	36.	D	61.	B		
13.	C	37.	C	62.	B		
14.	B	38.	D	63.	B		
15.	A	39.	D	64.	B		
16.	A	40.	B	65.	A		
17.	B	41.	A	66.	B		
18.	C	42.	B	67.	D		
19.	D	43.	D	68.	C		
20.	D	44.	A	69.	D		
21.	B	45.	C	70.	B		
22.	A	46.	C	71.	C		
23.	C	47.	D	72.	C		
24.	C	48.	B	73.	B		
25.	B	49.	B				

Rigor Analysis Table

Easy	21%	1,8,10,15,20,24,33,35,37,50,52,54,57,59,67,71,75
Average Rigor	39%	2,4,6,7,9,13,14,18,22,27,28,29,30,31,34,38,40,42, 45,47,51,55,56,58,63,64,66,74,76,78,79
Rigorous	40%	3,5,11,12,16,17,19,21,23,25,26,32,36,39,41,43,44, 46,48,49,53,60,61,62,65,68,69,70,72,73,77,80

Rationales with Sample Questions

1. **Which statement best describes a valid approach to testing a scientific hypothesis?**
   (Easy)

   A. Use computer simulations to verify the hypothesis

   B. Perform a mathematical analysis of the hypothesis

   C. Design experiments to test the hypothesis

   D. All of the above

Answer: D

Each of the answers A, B and C can have a crucial part in testing a scientific hypothesis. Although experiments may hold more weight than mathematical or computer-based analysis, these latter two methods of analysis can be critical, especially when experimental design is highly time consuming or financially costly.

2. **Which description best describes the role of a scientific model of a physical phenomenon?**
   (Average Rigor)

   A. An explanation that provides a reasonably accurate approximation of the phenomenon

   B. A theoretical explanation that describes exactly what is taking place

   C. A purely mathematical formulation of the phenomenon

   D. A predictive tool that has no interest in what is actually occurring

Answer: A

A scientific model seeks to provide the most fundamental and accurate description possible for physical phenomena, but, given the fact that natural science takes an *a posteriori* approach, models are always tentative and must be treated with some amount of skepticism. As a result, A is a better answer than B. Answers C and D overly emphasize one or another aspect of a model, rather than a synthesis of a number of aspects (such as a mathematical and predictive aspect).

3. **Which situation calls might best be described as involving an ethical dilemma for a scientist?**
    (Rigorous)

    A. Submission to a peer-review journal of a paper that refutes an established theory

    B. Synthesis of a new radioactive isotope of an element

    C. Use of a computer for modeling a newly-constructed nuclear reactor

    D. Use of a pen-and-paper approach to a difficult problem

Answer: B

Although answer A may be controversial, it does not involve an inherently ethical dilemma, since there is nothing unethical about presenting new information if it is true or valid. Answer C, likewise, has no necessary ethical dimension, as is the case with D. Synthesis of radioactive material, however, involves an ethical dimension with regard to the potential impact of the new isotope on the health of others and on the environment. The potential usefulness of such an isotope in weapons development is another ethical consideration.

4. **Which of the following is not a key purpose for the use of open communication about and peer-review of the results of scientific investigations?**
    (Average Rigor)

    A. Testing, by other scientists, of the results of an investigation for the purpose of refuting any evidence contrary to an established theory

    B. Testing, by other scientists, of the results of an investigation for the purpose of finding or eliminating any errors in reasoning or measurement

    C. Maintaining an open, public process to better promote honesty and integrity in science

    D. Provide a forum to help promote progress through mutual sharing and review of the results of investigations

Answer: A

Answers B, C and D all are important rationales for the use of open communication and peer-review in science. Answer A, however, would suggest that the purpose of these processes is to simply maintain the status quo; the history of science, however, suggests that this cannot and should not be the case.

5.   **Which of the following aspects of the use of computers for collecting experimental data is not a concern for the scientist?**
     (Rigorous)

   A. The relative speeds of the processor, peripheral, memory storage unit and any other components included in data acquisition equipment

   B. The financial cost of the equipment, utilities and maintenance

   C. Numerical error due to a lack of infinite precision in digital equipment

   D. The order of complexity of data analysis algorithms

Answer: D

Although answer D might be a concern for later, when actual analysis of the data is undertaken, the collection of data typically does not suffer from this problem. The use of computers does, however, pose problems when, for example, a peripheral collects data at a rate faster than the computer can process it (A), or if the cost of running the equipment or of purchasing the equipment is prohibitive (B). Numerical error is always a concern with any digital data acquisition system, since the data that is collected is never exact.

6.   **If a particular experimental observation contradicts a theory, what is the most appropriate approach that a physicist should take?**
      (Average Rigor)

      A. Immediately reject the theory and begin developing a new theory that better fits the observed results

      B. Report the experimental result in the literature without further ado

      C. Repeat the observations and check the experimental apparatus for any potential faulty components or human error, and then compare the results once more with the theory

      D. Immediately reject the observation as in error due to its conflict with theory

Answer: C

When experimental results contradict a reigning physical theory, as they do from time to time, it is almost never appropriate to immediately reject the theory (A) *or* the observational results (D). Also, since this is the case, reporting the result in the literature, without further analysis to provide an adequate explanation of the discrepancy, is unwise and unwarranted. Further testing is appropriate to determine whether the experiment is repeatable and whether any equipment or human errors have occurred. Only after further testing may the physicist begin to analyze the implications of the observational result.

7.   **Which of the following is *not* an SI unit?**
      (Average Rigor)

      A. Joule

      B. Coulomb

      C. Newton

      D. Erg

Answer: D

The first three responses are the SI (*Le Système International d'Unités*) units for energy, charge and force, respectively. The fourth answer, the erg, is the CGS (centimeter-gram-second) unit of energy.

8. **Which of the following best describes the relationship of precision and accuracy in scientific measurements?**
   (Easy)

   A. Accuracy is how well a particular measurement agrees with the value of the actual parameter being measured; precision is how well a particular measurement agrees with the average of other measurements taken for the same value

   B. Precision is how well a particular measurement agrees with the value of the actual parameter being measured; accuracy is how well a particular measurement agrees with the average of other measurements taken for the same value

   C. Accuracy is the same as precision

   D. Accuracy is a measure of numerical error; precision is a measure of human error

Answer: A

The accuracy of a measurement is how close the measurement is to the "true" value of the parameter being measured. Precision is how closely a group of measurements is to the mean value of all the measurements. By analogy, accuracy is how close a measurement is to the center of the bulls-eye, and precision is how tight a group is formed by multiple measurements, regardless of accuracy. Thus, measurements may be very precise and not very accurate, or they may be accurate but not overly precise, or they may be both or neither.

9. **Which statement best describes a rationale for the use of statistical analysis in characterizing the numerical results of a scientific experiment or investigation?**
   (Average Rigor)

   A. Experimental results need to be adjusted, through the use of statistics, to conform to theoretical predictions and computer models

   B. Since experiments are prone to a number of errors and uncertainties, statistical analysis provides a method for characterizing experimental measurements by accounting for or quantifying these undesirable effects

   C. Experiments are not able to provide any useful information, and statistical analysis is needed to impose a theoretical framework on the results

   D. Statistical analysis is needed to relate experimental measurements to computer-simulated values

Answer: B

One of the main reasons for the use of statistical analysis is that various types of noise, errors and uncertainties can easily enter into experimental results. Among other things, statistics can help alleviate these difficulties by quantifying an average measurement value and a variance or standard deviation of the set of measurements. This helps determine the accuracy and precision of a set of experimental results. Answers A, C and D do not accurately describe ideal scientific experiments or the use of statistics.

10. **Which statement best characterizes the relationship of mathematics and experimentation in physics?**
    (Easy)

    A. Experimentation has no bearing on the mathematical models that are developed for physical phenomena

    B. Mathematics is a tool that assists in the development of models for various physical phenomena as they are studied experimentally, with observations of the phenomena being a test of the validity of the mathematical model

    C. Mathematics is used to test the validity of experimental apparatus for physical measurements

    D. Mathematics is an abstract field with no relationship to concrete experimentation

Answer: B

Mathematics is used extensively in the study of physics for creating models of various phenomena. Since mathematics is abstract and not necessarily tied to physical reality, it must be tempered by experimental results. Although a particular theory may be mathematically elegant, it may have no explanatory power due to its inability to account for certain aspects of physical reality, or due to its inclusion of gratuitous aspects that seem to have no physical analog. Thus, experimentation is foundational, with mathematics being a tool for organizing and providing a greater context for observational results.

11. **Which of the following mathematical tools would not typically be used for the analysis of an electromagnetic phenomenon?**
    (Rigorous)

    A. Trigonometry

    B. Vector calculus

    C. Group theory

    D. Numerical methods

Answer: C

Trigonometry and vector calculus are both key tools for solving problems in electromagnetics. These are, primarily, analytical methods, although they play a part in numerical analysis as well. Numerical methods are helpful for many problems that are otherwise intractable analytically. Group theory, although it may have some applications in certain highly specific areas, is generally not used in the study of electromagnetics.

12. **For a problem that involves parameters that vary in rate with direction and location, which of the following mathematical tools would most likely be of greatest value?**
(*Rigorous*)

    A. Trigonometry

    B. Numerical analysis

    C. Group theory

    D. Vector calculus

Answer: D

Each of the above answers might have some value for individual problems, but, generally speaking, those problems that deal with quantities that have direction and magnitude (vectors), and that deal with rates, would most likely be amenable to analysis using vector calculus (D).

13. **Which of the following devices would be best suited for an experiment designed to measure alpha particle emissions from a sample?**
(*Average Rigor*)

    A. Photomultiplier tube

    B. Thermocouple

    C. Geiger-Müller tube

    D. Transistor

Answer: C

The Geiger-Müller tube is the main component of the so-called Geiger counter, which is designed specifically for detecting ionizing radiation emissions, including alpha particles. The photomultiplier tube is better suited to measurement of electromagnetic radiation closer to the visible range (A), and the thermocouple is better suited to measurement of temperature (B). Transistors may be involved in instrumentation, but they are not sensors.

14. **Which of the following experiments presents the most likely cause for concern about laboratory safety?**
    (Average Rigor)

> A. Computer simulation of a nuclear reactor
>
> B. Vibration measurement with a laser
>
> C. Measurement of fluorescent light intensity with a battery-powered photodiode circuit
>
> D. Ambient indoor ionizing radiation measurement with a Geiger counter.

Answer: B

Assuming no profoundly foolish acts, the use of a computer for simulation (A), measurement with a battery-powered photodiode circuit (C) and ambient radiation measurement (D) pose no particular hazards. The use of a laser (B) must be approached with care, however, as unintentional reflections or a lack of sufficient protection can cause permanent eye damage.

15. **A brick and hammer fall from a ledge at the same time. They would be expected to:**
    (Easy)

> A. Reach the ground at the same time
>
> B. Accelerate at different rates due to difference in weight
>
> C. Accelerate at different rates due to difference in potential energy
>
> D. Accelerate at different rates due to difference in kinetic energy

Answer: A

This is a classic question about falling in a gravitational field. All objects are acted upon equally by gravity, so they should reach the ground at the same time. (In real life, air resistance can make a difference, but not at small heights for similarly shaped objects.) In any case, weight, potential energy, and kinetic energy do not affect gravitational acceleration. Thus, the only possible answer is (A).

16. **A baseball is thrown with an initial velocity of 30 m/s at an angle of 45°. Neglecting air resistance, how far away will the ball land?** *(Rigorous)*

    A. 92 m

    B. 78 m

    C. 65 m

    D. 46 m

Answer: A

To answer this question, recall the equations for projectile motion:
$y = \frac{1}{2} a t^2 + v_{0y} t + y_0$
$x = v_{0x} t + x_0$
where x and y are horizontal and vertical position, respectively; t is time; a is acceleration due to gravity; v_{0x} and v_{0y} are initial horizontal and vertical velocity, respectively; x_0 and y_0 are initial horizontal and vertical position, respectively.
For our case:
x_0 and y_0 can be set to zero
both v_{0x} and v_{0y} are (using trigonometry) = $(\sqrt{2} / 2)$ 30 m/s
$a = -9.81$ m/s^2

We then use the vertical motion equation to find the time aloft (setting y equal to zero to find the solution for t):
$0 = \frac{1}{2} (-9.81$ m/s$^2) t^2 + (\sqrt{2} / 2)$ 30 m/s t
Then solving, we find:
t = 0 s (initial set-up) or t = 4.324 s (time to go up and down)

Using t = 4.324 s in the horizontal motion equation, we find:
$x = ((\sqrt{2} / 2)$ 30 m/s) (4.324 s)
$x = 91.71$ m

This is consistent only with answer (A).

17. **A skateboarder accelerates down a ramp, with constant acceleration of two meters per second squared, from rest. The distance in meters, covered after four seconds, is:**
    (Rigorous)

    A. 10

    B. 16

    C. 23

    D. 37

Answer: B

To answer this question, recall the equation relating constant acceleration to distance and time:
$x = \frac{1}{2} a t^2 + v_0 t + x_0$ where x is position; a is acceleration; t is time; v_0 and x_0 are initial velocity and position (both zero in this case)

thus, to solve for x:
$x = \frac{1}{2} (2 \text{ m/s}^2) (4^2 \text{s}^2) + 0 + 0$
$x = 16$ m

This is consistent only with answer (B).

18. **When acceleration is plotted versus time, the area under the graph represents:**
    (Average Rigor)

    A. Time

    B. Distance

    C. Velocity

    D. Acceleration

Answer: C
The area under a graph will have units equal to the product of the units of the two axes. (To visualize this, picture a graphed rectangle with its area equal to length times width.)
Therefore, multiply units of acceleration by units of time:
(length/time^2)(time)
This equals length/time, i.e. units of velocity.

19. An inclined plane is tilted by gradually increasing the angle of elevation θ, until the block will slide down at a constant velocity. The coefficient of friction, μ_k, is given by:
    (Rigorous)

    A. cos θ

    B. sin θ

    C. cosecant θ

    D. tangent θ

Answer: D

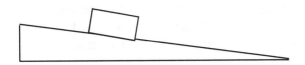

When the block moves, its force upstream (due to friction) must equal its force downstream (due to gravity).

The friction force is given by
$F_f = \mu_k N$
where μ_k is the friction coefficient and N is the normal force.

Using similar triangles, the gravity force is given by
$F_g = mg \sin \theta$
and the normal force is given by
$N = mg \cos \theta$

When the block moves at constant velocity, it must have zero net force, so set equal the force of gravity and the force due to friction:
$F_f = F_g$
$\mu_k \, mg \cos \theta = mg \sin \theta$
$\mu_k = \tan \theta$

Answer (D) is the only appropriate choice in this case.

20. An object traveling through air loses part of its energy of motion due to friction. Which statement best describes what has happened to this energy?
(*Easy*)

    A. The energy is destroyed

    B. The energy is converted to static charge

    C. The energy is radiated as electromagnetic waves

    D. The energy is lost to heating of the air

Answer: D

Since energy must be conserved, the energy of motion of the object is converted, in part, to energy of motion of the molecules in the air (and, to some extent, in the object). This additional motion is equivalent to an increase in heat. Thus, friction is a loss of energy of motion through heating.

21. The weight of an object on the earth's surface is designated x. When it is two earth's radii from the surface of the earth, its weight will be:
(*Rigorous*)

    A. $x/4$

    B. $x/9$

    C. $4x$

    D. $16x$

Answer: B

To solve this problem, apply the universal Law of Gravitation to the object and Earth:

$F_{gravity} = (GM_1M_2)/R^2$
Because the force of gravity varies with the square of the radius between the objects, the force (or weight) on the object will be decreased by the square of the multiplication factor on the radius. Note that the object on Earth's surface is *already* at one radius from Earth's center. Thus, when it is two radii from Earth's surface, it is three radii from Earth's center. R^2 is then nine, so the weight is $x/9$. Only answer (B) matches these calculations.

22. **Which of the following units is not used to measure torque?**
    (Average Rigor)

    A. slug ft

    B. lb ft

    C. N m

    D. dyne cm

Answer: A

To answer this question, recall that torque is always calculated by multiplying units of force by units of distance. Therefore, answer (A), which is the product of units of mass and units of distance, must be the choice of incorrect units. Indeed, the other three answers all could measure torque, since they are of the correct form. It is a good idea to review "English Units" before the teacher test, because they are occasionally used in problems.

23. A uniform pole weighing 100 grams, that is one meter in length, is supported by a pivot at 40 centimeters from the left end. In order to maintain static position, a 200 gram mass must be placed _____ centimeters from the left end.
    (Rigorous)

    A. 10

    B. 45

    C. 35

    D. 50

Answer: C

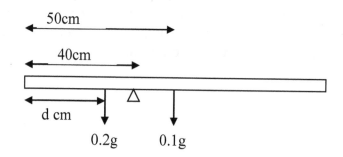

Since the pole is uniform, we can assume that its weight 0.1g acts at the center, i.e. 50 cm from the left end. In order to keep the pole balanced on the pivot, the 200 gram mass must be placed such that the torque on the pole due to the mass is equal and opposite to the torque due to the pole's weight. Thus, if the 200 gram mass is placed d cm from the left end of the pole,

$(40 - d) \times 0.2g = 10 \times 0.1g$; $40 - d = 5$; $d = 35$ cm

24. **The magnitude of a force is:**
    (Easy)

   A. Directly proportional to mass and inversely to acceleration

   B. Inversely proportional to mass and directly to acceleration

   C. Directly proportional to both mass and acceleration

   D. Inversely proportional to both mass and acceleration

Answer: C

To solve this problem, recall Newton's 2nd Law, i.e. net force is equal to mass times acceleration. Therefore, the only possible answer is (C).

25. **A projectile with a mass of 1.0 kg has a muzzle velocity of 1500.0 m/s when it is fired from a cannon with a mass of 500.0 kg. If the cannon slides on a frictionless track, it will recoil with a velocity of _____ m/s.**
    (Rigorous)

   A. 2.4

   B. 3.0

   C. 3.5

   D. 1500

Answer: B

To solve this problem, apply Conservation of Momentum to the cannon-projectile system. The system is initially at rest, with total momentum of 0 kg m/s. Since the cannon slides on a frictionless track, we can assume that the net momentum stays the same for the system. Therefore, the momentum forward (of the projectile) must equal the momentum backward (of the cannon). Thus:

$p_{projectile} = p_{cannon}$

$m_{projectile} \, v_{projectile} = m_{cannon} \, v_{cannon}$

(1.0 kg)(1500.0 m/s) = (500.0 kg)(x)

$x = 3.0$ m/s

Only answer (B) matches these calculations.

26. A car (mass m_1) is driving at velocity v, when it smashes into an unmoving car (mass m_2), locking bumpers. Both cars move together at the same velocity. The common velocity will be given by: (*Rigorous*)

   A. m_1v/m_2

   B. m_2v/m_1

   C. $m_1v/(m_1 + m_2)$

   D. $(m_1 + m_2)v/m_1$

Answer: C

In this problem, there is an inelastic collision, so the best method is to assume that momentum is conserved. (Recall that momentum is equal to the product of mass and velocity.)
Therefore, apply Conservation of Momentum to the two-car system:
Momentum at Start = Momentum at End
(Mom. of Car 1) + (Mom. of Car 2) = (Mom. of 2 Cars Coupled)
$m_1v + 0 = (m_1 + m_2)x$
$x = m_1v/(m_1 + m_2)$
Only answer (C) matches these calculations.

Watch out for the other answers, because errors in algebra could lead to a match with incorrect answer (D), and assumption of an elastic collision could lead to a match with incorrect answer (A).

27. **A satellite is in a circular orbit above the earth. Which statement is false?**
(Average Rigor)

   A. An external force causes the satellite to maintain orbit.

   B. The satellite's inertia causes it to maintain orbit.

   C. The satellite is accelerating toward the earth.

   D. The satellite's velocity and acceleration are not in the same direction.

Answer: B

To answer this question, recall that in circular motion, an object's inertia tends to keep it moving straight (tangent to the orbit), so a centripetal force (leading to centripetal acceleration) must be applied. In this case, the centripetal force is gravity due to the earth, which keeps the object in motion. Thus, (A), (C), and (D) are true, and (B) is the only false
statement.

28. **A 100 g mass revolving around a fixed point, on the end of a 0.5 meter string, circles once every 0.25 seconds. What is the magnitude of the centripetal acceleration?**
(Average Rigor)

   A. $1.23 \ m/s^2$

   B. $31.6 \ m/s^2$

   C. $100 \ m/s^2$

   D. $316 \ m/s^2$

Answer: D

The centripetal acceleration is equal to the product of the radius and the square of the angular frequency ω. In this case, ω is equal to 25.1 Hz. Squaring this value and multiplying by 0.5 m yields the result in answer D.

29. **Which statement best describes the relationship of simple harmonic motion to a simple pendulum of length L, mass m and displacement of arc length s?**
(Average Rigor)

   A. A simple pendulum cannot be modeled using simple harmonic motion

   B. A simple pendulum may be modeled using the same expression as Hooke's law for displacement s, but with a spring constant equal to the tension on the string

   C. A simple pendulum may be modeled using the same expression as Hooke's law for displacement s, but with a spring constant equal to m g/L

   D. A simple pendulum typically does not undergo simple harmonic motion

Answer: C

The force on a simple pendulum may be expressed approximately (when displacement s is small) according to the following equation:

$$F \approx -\frac{mg}{L}s$$

This expression has the same form as Hooke's law (F = -kx). Thus, answer C is the most correct response. Another approach to the question is to eliminate answers A and D as obviously incorrect, and then to eliminate answer B as not having appropriate units for the spring constant.

30. **A mass of 2 kg connected to a spring undergoes simple harmonic motion at a frequency of 3 Hz. What is the spring constant?**
    (Average Rigor)

    A. 6 kg/s^2

    B. 18 kg/s^2

    C. 710 kg/s^2

    D. 1000 kg/s^2

Answer: C

The spring constant, k, is equal to mω^2. In this case, ω is equal to 2π times the frequency of 3 Hz. The spring constant may be derived quickly by recognizing that the position of the mass varies sinusoidally with time at an angular frequency ω. Noting that the acceleration is the second derivative of the position with respect to time, the expression for k in Hooke's law (F = -kx) can be easily derived.

31. **The kinetic energy of an object is _____ proportional to its _____.**
    (Average Rigor)

    A. Inversely...inertia

    B. Inversely...velocity

    C. Directly...mass

    D. Directly...time

Answer: C

To answer this question, recall that kinetic energy is equal to one-half of the product of an object's mass and the square of its velocity:
KE = ½ m v^2

Therefore, kinetic energy is directly proportional to mass, and the answer is (C). Note that although kinetic energy is associated with both velocity and momentum (a measure of inertia), it is not *inversely* proportional to either one.

32.   A force is given by the vector 5 N x + 3 N y (where x and y are the
        unit vectors for the x- and y- axes, respectively). This force is
        applied to move a 10 kg object 5 m, in the x direction. How much
        work was done?
        (Rigorous)

        A. 250 J

        B. 400 J

        C. 40 J

        D. 25 J

Answer: D

To find out how much work was done, note that work counts only the force in the
direction of motion. Therefore, the only part of the vector that we use is the 5 N
in the x-direction. Note, too, that the mass of the object is not relevant in this
problem. We use the work equation:
Work = (Force in direction of motion) (Distance moved)
Work = (5 N) (5 m)
Work = 25 J
This is consistent only with answer (D).

33.   An office building entry ramp uses the principle of which simple
        machine?
        (Easy)

        A. Lever

        B. Pulley

        C. Wedge

        D. Inclined Plane

Answer: D

To answer this question, recall the definitions of the various simple machines. A
ramp, which trades a longer traversed distance for a shallower slope, is an
example of an Inclined Plane, consistent with answer (D). Levers and Pulleys
act to change size and/or direction of an input force, which is not relevant here.
Wedges apply the same force over a smaller area, increasing pressure—again,
not relevant in this case.

34.   If the internal energy of a system remains constant, how much work
        is done by the system if 1 kJ of heat energy is added?
        (Average Rigor)

           A. 0 kJ

           B. -1 kJ

           C. 1 kJ

           D. 3.14 kJ

Answer: C

According to the first law of thermodynamics, if the internal energy of a system
remains constant, then any heat energy added to the system must be balanced
by the system performing work on its surroundings. In the case of an ideal gas,
the gas would necessarily expand when heated, assuming a constant internal
energy was somehow maintained. Applying conservation of energy, answer C is
found to be correct.

35.   A calorie is the amount of heat energy that will:
        (Easy)

           A. Raise the temperature of one gram of water from 14.5° C to 15.5°
              C.

           B. Lower the temperature of one gram of water from 16.5° C to 15.5°
              C

           C. Raise the temperature of one gram of water from 32° F to 33° F

           D. Cause water to boil at two atmospheres of pressure.

Answer: A

The definition of a calorie is, "the amount of energy to raise one gram of water by
one degree Celsius," and so answer (A) is correct. Do not get confused by the
fact that 14.5° C seems like a random number. Also, note that answer (C) tries to
confuse you with degrees Fahrenheit, which are irrelevant to this problem.

36. Use the information on heats below to solve this problem. An ice block at 0° Celsius is dropped into 100 g of liquid water at 18° Celsius. When thermal equilibrium is achieved, only liquid water at 0° Celsius is left. What was the mass, in grams, of the original block of ice?

Given: Heat of fusion of ice = 80 cal/g
Heat of vaporization of ice = 540 cal/g
Specific Heat of ice = 0.50 cal/g°C
Specific Heat of water = 1 cal/g°C

(*Rigorous*)

A. 2.0

B. 5.0

C. 10.0

D. 22.5

Answer: D

To solve this problem, apply Conservation of Energy to the ice-water system. Any gain of heat to the melting ice must be balanced by loss of heat in the liquid water. Use the two equations relating temperature, mass, and energy:
$Q = m\,C\,\Delta T$ (for heat loss/gain from change in temperature)
$Q = m\,L$ (for heat loss/gain from phase change)
where Q is heat change; m is mass; C is specific heat; ΔT is change in temperature; L is heat of phase change (in this case, melting, also known as "fusion").

Then
$Q_{\text{ice to water}} = Q_{\text{water to ice}}$
(Note that the ice only melts; it stays at 0° Celsius—otherwise, we would have to include a term for warming the ice as well. Also the information on the heat of vaporization for water is irrelevant to this problem.)
$m\,L = m\,C\,\Delta T$
$x\,(80 \text{ cal/g}) = 100g\ 1cal/g°C\ 18°C$
$x\,(80 \text{ cal/g}) = 1800 \text{ cal}$
$x = 22.5 \text{ g}$

Only answer (D) matches this result.

37.   **Heat transfer by electromagnetic waves is termed:**
       (Easy)

           A. Conduction

           B. Convection

           C. Radiation

           D. Phase Change

Answer: C

To answer this question, recall the different ways that heat is transferred. Conduction is the transfer of heat through direct physical contact and molecules moving and hitting each other. Convection is the transfer of heat via density differences and flow of fluids. Radiation is the transfer of heat via electromagnetic waves (and can occur in a vacuum). Phase Change causes transfer of heat (though not of temperature) in order for the molecules to take their new phase. This is consistent, therefore, only with answer (C).

38.   **A cooking thermometer in an oven works because the metals it is composed of have different:**
       (Average Rigor)

           A. Melting points

           B. Heat convection

           C. Magnetic fields

           D. Coefficients of expansion

Answer: D

A thermometer of the type that can withstand oven temperatures works by having more than one metal strip. These strips expand at different rates with temperature increases, causing the dial to register the new temperature. This is consistent only with answer (D). If you did not know how an oven thermometer works, you could still omit the incorrect answers: It is unlikely that the metals in a thermometer would melt in the oven to display the temperature; the magnetic fields would not be useful information in this context; heat convection applies in fluids, not solids.

39. **Which of the following is not an assumption upon which the kinetic-molecular theory of gases is based?**
(Rigorous)

A. Quantum mechanical effects may be neglected

B. The particles of a gas may be treated statistically

C. The particles of the gas are treated as very small masses

D. Collisions between gas particles and container walls are inelastic

Answer: D

Since the kinetic-molecular theory is classical in nature, quantum mechanical effects are indeed ignored, and answer A is incorrect. The theory also treats gases as a statistical collection of point-like particles with finite masses. As a result, answers B and C may also be eliminated. Thus, answer D is correct: collisions between gas particles and container walls are treated as elastic in the kinetic-molecular theory.

40. **What is temperature?**
(Average Rigor)

A. Temperature is a measure of the conductivity of the atoms or molecules in a material

B. Temperature is a measure of the kinetic energy of the atoms or molecules in a material

C. Temperature is a measure of the relativistic mass of the atoms or molecules in a material

D. Temperature is a measure of the angular momentum of electrons in a material

Answer: B

Temperature is, in fact, a measure of the kinetic energy of the constituent components of a material. Thus, as a material is heated, the atoms or molecules that compose it acquire greater energy of motion. This increased motion results in the breaking of chemical bonds and in an increase in disorder, thus leading to melting or vaporizing of the material at sufficiently high temperatures.

41. **Solids expand when heated because:**
(Rigorous)

    A. Molecular motion causes expansion

    B. $PV = nRT$

    C. Magnetic forces stretch the chemical bonds

    D. All material is effectively fluid

Answer: A

When any material is heated, the heat energy becomes energy of motion for the material's molecules. This increased motion causes the material to expand (or sometimes to change phase). Therefore, the answer is (A). Answer (B) is the ideal gas law, which gives a relationship between temperature, pressure, and volume for gases. Answer (C) is a red herring (misleading answer that is untrue). Answer (D) may or may not be true, but it is not the best answer to this question.

42. **What should be the behavior of an electroscope, which has been grounded in the presence of a positively charged object (1), after the ground connection is removed and then the charged object is removed from the vicinity (2)?**
(Average Rigor)

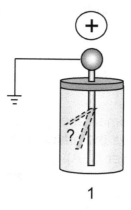

1   2

A. The metal leaf will start deflected (1) and then relax to an undeflected position (2)

B. The metal leaf will start in an undeflected position (1) and then be deflected (2)

C. The metal leaf will remain undeflected in both cases

D. The metal leaf will be deflected in both cases

Answer: B

When grounded, the electroscope will show no deflection. Nevertheless, if the ground is then removed and the charged object taken from the vicinity (in that order), the excess charge that existed near the sphere of the electroscope will distribute itself throughout the instrument, resulting in an overall net excess charge that will deflect the metal leaf.

43. **The electric force in Newtons, on two small objects (each charged to –10 microCoulombs and separated by 2 meters) is:**
    (Rigorous)

    A. 1.0

    B. 9.81

    C. 31.0

    D. 0.225

Answer: D

To answer this question, use Coulomb's Law, which gives the electric force between two charged particles:

$F = k Q_1 Q_2 / r^2$

Then our unknown is F, and our knowns are:

$k = 9.0 \times 10^9 \ Nm^2/C^2$

$Q_1 = Q_2 = -10 \times 10^{-6} \ C$

$r = 2 \ m$

Therefore

$F = (9.0 \times 10^9)(-10 \times 10^{-6})(-10 \times 10^{-6})/(2^2) \ N$

$F = 0.225 \ N$

This is compatible only with answer (D).

44. **A 10 ohm resistor and a 50 ohm resistor are connected in parallel. If the current in the 10 ohm resistor is 5 amperes, the current (in amperes) running through the 50 ohm resistor is:**
   (Rigorous)

   A. 1

   B. 50

   C. 25

   D. 60

Answer: A

To answer this question, use Ohm's Law, which relates voltage to current and resistance:
V = IR
where V is voltage; I is current; R is resistance.

We also use the fact that in a parallel circuit, the voltage is the same across the branches.

Because we are given that in one branch, the current is 5 amperes and the resistance is 10 ohms, we deduce that the voltage in this circuit is their product, 50 volts (from V = IR).

We then use V = IR again, this time to find I in the second branch. Because V is 50 volts, and R is 50 ohm, we calculate that I has to be 1 ampere.

This is consistent only with answer (A).

45. **How much power is dissipated through the following resistive circuit?**
    (Average Rigor)

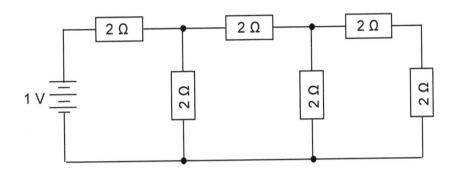

A. 0 W

B. 0.22 W

C. 0.31 W

D. 0.49 W

Answer: C

Use the rules of series and parallel resistors to quickly form an equivalent circuit with a single voltage source and a single resistor. In this case, the equivalent resistance is 3.25 Ω. The power dissipated by the circuit is the square of the voltage divided by the resistance. The final answer is C.

46. **The greatest number of 100 watt lamps that can be connected in parallel with a 120 volt system without blowing a 5 amp fuse is: (Rigorous)**

    A. 24

    B. 12

    C. 6

    D. 1

Answer: C

To solve fuse problems, you must add together all the drawn current in the parallel branches, and make sure that it is less than the fuse's amp measure. Because we know that electrical power is equal to the product of current and voltage, we can deduce that:
$I = P/V$ (I = current (amperes); P = power (watts); V = voltage (volts))

Therefore, for each lamp, the current is 100/120 amperes, or 5/6 ampere. The highest possible number of lamps is thus six, because six lamps at 5/6 ampere each adds to 5 amperes; more will blow the fuse.

This is consistent only with answer (C).

47. **Which of the following statements may be taken as a legitimate inference based upon the Maxwell equation that states $\nabla \cdot \mathbf{B} = 0$? (Average Rigor)**

    A. The electric and magnetic fields are decoupled

    B. The electric and magnetic fields are mediated by the W boson

    C. There are no photons

    D. There are no magnetic monopoles

Answer: D

Since the divergence of the magnetic flux density is always zero, there cannot be any magnetic monopoles (charges), given this Maxwell equation. If Gauss's law is applied to magnetic flux in the same manner as it is to electric flux, then the total magnetic "charge" contained within any closed surface must always be zero. This is another way of viewing the problem. Thus, answer D is correct. This answer may also be chosen by elimination of the other statements, which are untenable.

48. **What effect might an applied external magnetic field have on the magnetic domains of a ferromagnetic material?**
    (Rigorous)

    A. The domains that are not aligned with the external field increase in size, but those that are aligned decrease in size

    B. The domains that are not aligned with the external field decrease in size, but those that are aligned increase in size

    C. The domains align perpendicular to the external field

    D. There is no effect on the magnetic domains

Answer: B

Recall that ferromagnetic domains are portions of a magnetic material that have a local magnetic moment. The material may have an overall lack of a magnetic moment due to random alignment of its domains. In the presence of an applied field, the domains may align with the field to some extent, or the boundaries of the domains may shift to give greater weight to those domains that are aligned with the field, at the expense of those domains that are not aligned with the field. As a result, of the possibilities above, B is the best answer.

49.	What is the effect of running current in the same direction along two parallel wires, as shown below?
(Rigorous)

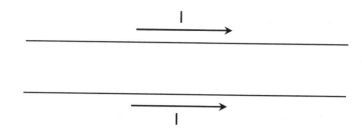

A. There is no effect

B. The wires attract one another

C. The wires repel one another

D. A torque is applied to both wires

Answer: B

Since the direction of the force on a current element is proportional to the cross product of the direction of the current element and the magnetic field, there is either an attractive or repulsive force between the two wires shown above. Using the right hand rule, it can be found that the magnetic field on the top wire due to the bottom wire is directed out of the plane of the page. Performing the cross product shows that the force on the upper wire is directed toward the lower wire. A similar argument can be used for the lower wire. Thus, the correct answer is B: an attractive force is exerted on the wires.

50. **The current induced in a coil is defined by which of the following laws?**
(*Easy*)

    A. Lenz's Law

    B. Burke's Law

    C. The Law of Spontaneous Combustion

    D. Snell's Law

Answer: A

Lenz's Law states that an induced electromagnetic force always gives rise to a current whose magnetic field opposes the original flux change. There is no relevant "Snell's Law," "Burke's Law," or "Law of Spontaneous Combustion" in electromagnetism. (In fact, only Snell's Law is a real law of these three, and it refers to refracted light.) Therefore, the only appropriate answer is (A).

51. **A light bulb is connected in series with a rotating coil within a magnetic field. The brightness of the light may be increased by any of the following except:**
(*Average Rigor*)

    A. Rotating the coil more rapidly.

    B. Using more loops in the coil.

    C. Using a different color wire for the coil.

    D. Using a stronger magnetic field.

Answer: C

To answer this question, recall that the rotating coil in a magnetic field generates electric current, by Faraday's Law. Faraday's Law states that the amount of emf generated is proportional to the rate of change of magnetic flux through the loop. This increases if the coil is rotated more rapidly (A), if there are more loops (B), or if the magnetic field is stronger (D). Thus, the only answer to this question is (C).

52.   **What is the direction of the magnetic field at the center of the loop of current (I) shown below (i.e., at point A)?**
(Easy)

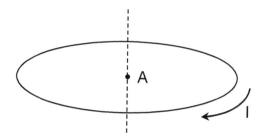

A. Down, along the axis (dotted line)

B. Up, along the axis (dotted line)

C. The magnetic field is oriented in a radial direction

D. There is no magnetic field at point A

Answer: A

The magnetic field may be found by applying the right-hand rule. The magnetic field curls around the wire in the direction of the curled fingers when the thumb is pointed in the direction of the current. Since there is a degree of symmetry, with point A lying in the center of the loop, the contributions of all the current elements on the loop must yield a field that is either directed up or down at the axis. Use of the right-hand rule indicates that the field is directed down. Thus, answer A is correct.

53. **The use of two circuits next to each other, with a change in current in the primary circuit, demonstrates:**
    (Rigorous)

    A. Mutual current induction

    B. Dielectric constancy

    C. Harmonic resonance

    D. Resistance variation

Answer: A

To answer this question, recall that changing current induces a change in magnetic flux, which in turn causes a change in current to oppose that change (Lenz's and Faraday's Laws). Thus, (A) is correct. If you did not remember that, note that harmonic resonance is irrelevant here (eliminating (C)), and there is no change in resistance in the circuits (eliminating (D)).

54. **A semi-conductor allows current to flow:**
    (Easy)

    A. Never

    B. Always

    C. As long as it stays below a maximum temperature

    D. When a minimum voltage is applied

Answer: D

To answer this question, recall that semiconductors do not conduct as well as conductors (eliminating answer (B)), but they conduct better than insulators (eliminating answer (A)). Semiconductors can conduct better when the temperature is higher (eliminating answer (C)), and their electrons move most readily under a potential difference. Thus the answer can only be (D).

55. **All of the following use semi-conductor technology, except a(n):**
    (Average Rigor)

    A. Transistor

    B. Diode

    C. Capacitor

    D. Operational Amplifier

Answer: C

Semi-conductor technology is used in transistors and operational amplifiers, and diodes are the basic unit of semi-conductors. Therefore the only possible answer is (C), and indeed a capacitor does not require semi-conductor technology.

56. **A wave generator is used to create a succession of waves. The rate of wave generation is one every 0.33 seconds. The period of these waves is:**
    (Average Rigor)

    A. 2.0 seconds

    B. 1.0 seconds

    C. 0.33 seconds

    D. 3.0 seconds

Answer: C

The definition of a period is the length of time between wave crests. Therefore, when waves are generated one per 0.33 seconds, that same time (0.33 seconds) is the period. This is consistent only with answer (C). Do not be trapped into calculating the number of waves per second, which might lead you to choose answer (D).

57. An electromagnetic wave propagates through a vacuum. Independent of its wavelength, it will move with constant: *(Easy)*

    A. Acceleration

    B. Velocity

    C. Induction

    D. Sound

Answer: B

Electromagnetic waves are considered always to travel at the speed of light, so answer (B) is correct. Answers (C) and (D) can be eliminated in any case, because induction is not relevant here, and sound does not travel in a vacuum.

58. A wave has speed 60 m/s and wavelength 30,000 m. What is the frequency of the wave? *(Average Rigor)*

    A. 2.0×10^{-3} Hz

    B. 60 Hz

    C. 5.0×10^{2} Hz

    D. 1.8×10^{6} Hz

Answer: A

To answer this question, recall that wave speed is equal to the product of wavelength and frequency. Thus:
60 m/s = (30,000 m) (frequency)
frequency = 2.0×10^{-3} Hz

This is consistent only with answer (A).

59.   **Rainbows are created by:**
      (Easy)

      A. Reflection, dispersion, and recombination

      B. Reflection, resistance, and expansion

      C. Reflection, compression, and specific heat

      D. Reflection, refraction, and dispersion

Answer: D

To answer this question, recall that rainbows are formed by light that goes through water droplets and is dispersed into its colors. This is consistent with both answers (A) and (D). Then note that refraction is important in bending the differently colored light waves, while recombination is not a relevant concept here. Therefore, the answer is (D).

60.   **Which of the following is *not* a legitimate explanation for refraction of light rays at boundaries between different media?**
      (Rigorous)

      A. Light seeks the path of least time between two different points

      B. Due to phase matching and other boundary conditions, plane waves travel in different directions on either side of the boundary, depending on the material parameters

      C. The electric and magnetic fields become decoupled at the boundary

      D. Light rays obey Snell's law

Answer: C

Even if the exact implications of each explanation are not known or understood, answer C can be chosen due to its plain incorrectness. The other responses involve more or less fundamental explanations for the refraction of light rays (which are equivalent to plane waves) at media boundaries.

61.   A stationary sound source produces a wave of frequency *F*. An observer at position A is moving toward the horn, while an observer at position B is moving away from the horn. Which of the following is true?
       (Rigorous)

       A. $F_A < F < F_B$

       B. $F_B < F < F_A$

       C. $F < F_A < F_B$

       D. $F_B < F_A < F$

Answer: B

To answer this question, recall the Doppler Effect. As a moving observer approaches a sound source, s/he intercepts wave fronts sooner than if s/he were standing still. Therefore, the wave fronts seem to be coming more frequently. Similarly, as an observer moves away from a sound source, the wave fronts take longer to reach him/her. Therefore, the wave fronts seem to be coming less frequently. Because of this effect, the frequency at B will seem lower than the original frequency, and the frequency at A will seem higher than the original frequency. The only answer consistent with this is (B). Note also, that even if you weren't sure of which frequency should be greater/smaller, you could still reason that A and B should have opposite effects, and be able to eliminate answer choices (C) and (D).

62. **A monochromatic ray of light passes from air to a thick slab of glass (n = 1.41) at an angle of 45° from the normal. At what angle does it leave the air/glass interface?**
    (Rigorous)

    A. 45°

    B. 30°

    C. 15°

    D. 55°

Answer: B

To solve this problem use Snell's Law:
$n_1 \sin\theta_1 = n_2 \sin\theta_2$ (where n_1 and n_2 are the indexes of refraction and θ_1 and θ_2 are the angles of incidence and refraction).

Then, since the index of refraction for air is 1.0, we deduce:
$1 \sin 45° = 1.41 \sin x$
$x = \sin^{-1} ((1/1.41) \sin 45°)$
$x = 30°$

This is consistent only with answer (B). Also, note that you could eliminate answers (A) and (D) in any case, because the refracted light will have to bend at a smaller angle when entering glass.

63.   **If one sound is ten decibels louder than another, the ratio of the intensity of the first to the second is:**
      (Average Rigor)

      A. 20:1

      B. 10:1

      C. 1:1

      D. 1:10

Answer: B

To answer this question, recall that a decibel is defined as ten times the log of the ratio of sound intensities:
(decibel measure) = $10 \log (I / I_0)$ where I_0 is a reference intensity.

Therefore, in our case,
(decibels of first sound) = (decibels of second sound) + 10
$10 \log (I_1 / I_0) = 10 \log (I_2 / I_0) + 10$
$10 \log I_1 - 10 \log I_0 = 10 \log I_2 - 10 \log I_0 + 10$
$10 \log I_1 - 10 \log I_2 = 10$
$\log (I_1 / I_2) = 1$
$I_1 / I_2 = 10$

This is consistent only with answer (B).
(Be careful not to get the two intensities confused with each other.)

64. **The velocity of sound is greatest in:**
     (Average Rigor)

     A. Water

     B. Steel

     C. Alcohol

     D. Air

Answer: B

Sound is a longitudinal wave, which means that it shakes its medium in a way that propagates as sound traveling. The speed of sound depends on both elastic modulus and density, but for a comparison of the above choices, the answer is always that sound travels faster through a solid like steel, than through liquids or gases. Thus, the answer is (B).

65. **A vibrating string's frequency is _____ proportional to the _____.**
     (Rigorous)

     A. Directly; Square root of the tension

     B. Inversely; Length of the string

     C. Inversely; Squared length of the string

     D. Inversely; Force of the plectrum

Answer: A

To answer this question, recall that
$f = (n\,v) / (2\,L)$ where f is frequency; v is velocity; L is length

and

$v = (F_{tension} / (m / L))^{\frac{1}{2}}$ where $F_{tension}$ is tension; m is mass; others as above

so

$f = (n / 2\,L)\,((F_{tension} / (m / L))^{\frac{1}{2}}\,)$

indicating that frequency is directly proportional to the square root of the tension force. This is consistent only with answer (A). Note that in the final frequency equation, there is an inverse relationship with the square root of the length (after canceling like terms). This is not one of the options, however.

66. Which of the following apparatus can be used to measure the wavelength of a sound produced by a tuning fork?
     (Average Rigor)

          A. A glass cylinder, some water, and iron filings

          B. A glass cylinder, a meter stick, and some water

          C. A metronome and some ice water

          D. A comb and some tissue

Answer: B

To answer this question, recall that a sound will be amplified if it is reflected back to cause positive interference. This is the principle behind musical instruments that use vibrating columns of air to amplify sound (e.g. a pipe organ). Therefore, presumably a person could put varying amounts of water in the cylinder, and hold the vibrating tuning fork above the cylinder in each case. If the tuning fork sound is amplified when put at the top of the column, then the length of the air space would be an integral multiple of the sound's wavelength. This experiment is consistent with answer (B). Although the experiment would be tedious, none of the other options for materials suggest a better alternative.

67. The highest energy is associated with:
     (Easy)

          A. UV radiation

          B. Yellow light

          C. Infrared radiation

          D. Gamma radiation

Answer: D

To answer this question, recall the electromagnetic spectrum. The highest energy (and therefore frequency) rays are those with the lowest wavelength, i.e. gamma rays. (In order of frequency from lowest to highest are: radio, microwave, infrared, red through violet visible light, ultraviolet, X-rays, gamma rays.) Thus, the only possible answer is (D). Note that even if you did not remember the spectrum, you could deduce that gamma radiation is considered dangerous and thus might have the highest energy.

68.   An object two meters tall is speeding toward a plane mirror at 10 m/s. What happens to the image as it nears the surface of the mirror? *(Rigorous)*

A.   It becomes inverted.

B.   The Doppler Effect must be considered.

C.   It remains two meters tall.

D.   It changes from a real image to a virtual image.

Answer: C

Note that the mirror is a plane mirror, so the image is always a virtual image of the same size as the object. If the mirror were concave, then the image would be inverted until the object came within the focal distance of the mirror. The Doppler Effect is not relevant here. Thus, the only possible answer is (C).

69.   Automobile mirrors that have a sign, "objects are closer than they appear" say so because: *(Rigorous)*

A.   The real image of an obstacle, through a converging lens, appears farther away than the object.

B.   The real or virtual image of an obstacle, through a converging mirror, appears farther away than the object.

C.   The real image of an obstacle, through a diverging lens, appears farther away than the object.

D.   The virtual image of an obstacle, through a diverging mirror, appears farther away than the object.

Answer: D

To answer this question, first eliminate answer choices (A) and (C), because we have a mirror, not a lens. Then draw ray diagrams for diverging (convex) and converging (concave) mirrors, and note that because the focal point of a diverging mirror is behind the surface, the image is smaller than the object. This creates the illusion that the object is farther away, and therefore (D) is the correct answer.

70.   **If an object is 20 cm from a convex lens whose focal length is 10 cm, the image is:**
   (Rigorous)

  A. Virtual and upright

  B. Real and inverted

  C. Larger than the object

  D. Smaller than the object

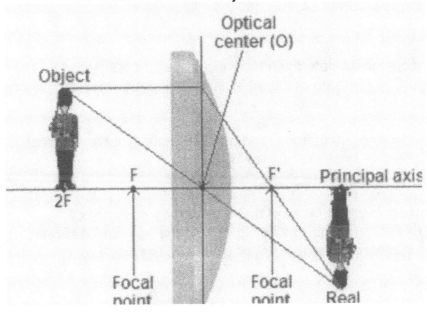

Answer: B

To solve this problem, draw a lens diagram with the lens, focal length, and image size.

The ray from the top of the object straight to the lens is focused through the far focus point; the ray from the top of the object through the near focus goes straight through the lens; the ray from the top of the object through the center of the lens continues. These three meet to form the "top" of the image, which is therefore real and inverted. This is consistent only with answer (B).

71. **The constant of proportionality between the energy and the frequency of electromagnetic radiation is known as the:**
   (Easy)

        A. Rydberg constant

        B. Energy constant

        C. Planck constant

        D. Einstein constant

Answer: C

Planck estimated his constant to determine the ratio between energy and frequency of radiation. The Rydberg constant is used to find the wavelengths of the visible lines on the hydrogen spectrum.

The other options are not relevant options, and may not actually have physical meaning. Therefore, the only possible answer is (C).

72. **Which phenomenon was first explained using the concept of quantization of energy, thus providing one of the key foundational principles for the later development of quantum theory?**
   (Rigorous)

        A. The photoelectric effect

        B. Time dilation

        C. Blackbody radiation

        D. Magnetism

Answer: C

Although the photoelectric effect applied principles of quantization in explaining the behavior of electrons emitted from a metallic surface when the surface is illuminated with electromagnetic radiation, the explanation of the phenomenon of blackbody radiation, provided by Max Planck, was the first major success of the concept of quantized energy. Magnetism may be explained quantum mechanically, but such an explanation was not forthcoming until well after Planck's quantization hypothesis. Time dilation is primarily explained through relativity theory.

73. **Which statement best describes why population inversion is
    necessary for a laser to operate?**
    (Rigorous)

    A. Population inversion prevents too many electrons from being
       excited into higher energy levels, thus preventing damage to the
       gain medium.

    B. Population inversion maintains a sufficient number of electrons in a
       higher energy state so as to allow a significant amount of
       stimulated emission.

    C. Population inversion prevents the laser from producing coherent
       light.

    D. Population inversion is not necessary for the operation of most
       lasers.

Answer: B

Population inversion is a state in which there are a larger number of electrons in
a particular higher-energy excited state than in a particular lower-energy state.
When perturbed by a passing photon, these electrons may then emit a photon of
the same energy (frequency) and phase. This is the process of stimulated
emission, which, when population inversion is obtained, can produce something
of a "chain reaction," thus giving lasers their characteristically monochromatic
and highly coherent light.

74. **Bohr's theory of the atom was the first to quantize:**
    (Average Rigor)

    A. Work

    B. Angular Momentum

    C. Torque

    D. Duality

Answer: B

Bohr was the first to quantize the angular momentum of electrons, as he
combined Rutherford's planet-style model with his knowledge of emerging
quantum theory. Recall that he derived a "quantum condition" for the single
electron, requiring electrons to exist at specific energy levels

75. **Two neutral isotopes of a chemical element have the same numbers of:**
(Easy)

    A. Electrons and Neutrons

    B. Electrons and Protons

    C. Protons and Neutrons

    D. Electrons, Neutrons, and Protons

Answer: B

To answer this question, recall that isotopes vary in their number of neutrons. (This fact alone eliminates answers (A), (C), and (D).) If you did not recall that fact, note that we are given that the two samples are of the same element, constraining the number of protons to be the same in each case. Then, use the fact that the samples are neutral, so the number of electrons must exactly balance the number of protons in each case. The only correct answer is thus (B).

76. **When a radioactive material emits an alpha particle only, its atomic number will:**
(Average Rigor)

    A. Decrease

    B. Increase

    C. Remain unchanged

    D. Change randomly

Answer: A

To answer this question, recall that in alpha decay, a nucleus emits the equivalent of a Helium atom. This includes two protons, so the original material changes its atomic number by a decrease of two.

77.   Ten grams of a sample of a radioactive material (half-life = 12 days) were stored for 48 days and re-weighed. The new mass of material was:
        (Rigorous)

        A. 1.25 g

        B. 2.5 g

        C. 0.83 g

        D. 0.625 g

Answer: D

To answer this question, note that 48 days is four half-lives for the material. Thus, the sample will degrade by half four times. At first, there are ten grams, then (after the first half-life) 5 g, then 2.5 g, then 1.25 g, and after the fourth half-life, there remains 0.625 g. You could also do the problem mathematically, by multiplying ten times $(\frac{1}{2})^4$, i.e. ½ for each half-life elapsed.

78.   Which of the following pairs of elements are not found to fuse in the centers of stars?
        (Average Rigor)

        A. Oxygen and Helium

        B. Carbon and Hydrogen

        C. Beryllium and Helium

        D. Cobalt and Hydrogen

Answer: D

To answer this question, recall that fusion is possible only when the final product has more binding energy than the reactants. Because binding energy peaks near a mass number of around 56, corresponding to Iron, any heavier elements would be unlikely to fuse in a typical star. (In very massive stars, there may be enough energy to fuse heavier elements.) Of all the listed elements, only Cobalt is heavier than iron, so answer (D) is correct.

79. **In a fission reactor, heavy water:**
     (Average Rigor)

      A. Cools off neutrons to control temperature

      B. Moderates fission reactions

      C. Initiates the reaction chain

      D. Dissolves control rods

Answer: B

In a nuclear reactor, heavy water is made up of oxygen atoms with hydrogen atoms called 'deuterium,' which contain two neutrons each. This allows the water to slow down (moderate) the neutrons, without absorbing many of them. This is consistent only with answer (B).

80. Given the following values for the masses of a proton, a neutron and an alpha particle, what is the nuclear binding energy of an alpha particle?
(*Rigorous*)

Proton mass = 1.6726 x 10^{-27} kg
Neutron mass = 1.6749 x 10^{-27} kg
Alpha particle mass = 6.6465 x 10^{-27} kg

    A. 0 J

    B. 7.3417 x 10^{-27} J

    C. 4 J

    D. 4.3589 x 10^{-12} J

Answer: D

The nuclear binding energy is the amount of energy that is required to break the nucleus into its component nucleons. In this case, the binding energy of an alpha particle, which is composed of two protons and two neutrons, is calculated by first finding the difference between the sum of the masses of all the nucleons and the mass of the alpha particle. Using the equation $E = mc^2$ to find the energy in terms of the mass difference of 4.85 x 10^{-29} kg, and using the speed of light of about 2.9979 x 10^8 m/s, the result is the value given in answer D.

CPSIA information can be obtained
at www.ICGtesting.com
Printed in the USA
BVHW050237261218
536369BV00010B/128